Gender Violence
and the Press

This series of publications on Africa, Latin America, and Southeast Asia is designed to present significant research, translation, and opinion to area specialists and to a wide community of persons interested in world affairs. The editor seeks manuscripts of quality on any subject and can generally make a decision regarding publication within three months of receipt of the original work. Production methods generally permit a work to appear within one year of acceptance. The editor works closely with authors to produce a high quality book. The series appears in a paperback format and is distributed worldwide. For more information, contact the executive editor at Ohio University Press, Scott Quadrangle, University Terrace, Athens, Ohio 45701.

Executive editor: Gillian Berchowitz
AREA CONSULTANTS
Africa: Diane Ciekawy
Latin America: Thomas Walker
Southeast Asia: James L. Cobban

Gender Violence and the Press

THE ST. KIZITO STORY

H. Leslie Steeves

Ohio University Center for International Studies
Monographs in International Studies
Africa Series No. 67
Athens

© 1997 by the
Center for International Studies
Ohio University
Printed in the United States of America
All rights reserved
03 02 01 00 99 98 97   5 4 3 2 1

The books in the Center for International Studies Monograph Series
are printed on acid-free paper ∞

Maps on page xvi of Kenya and Meru District. *Sources:* U.S. Central
Intelligence Agency, Kenya Base Edition 801061 (B00446) (Langeley,
Virginia: C.I.A., January 1988); Republic of Kenya, Development
Plan 1994–96 (Nairobi: Government Printer, 1994); Kenya Office of
the Vice President and Ministry of Planning and National Develop-
ment, Meru District Development Plan 1994–96 (Nairobi: Kenya
Office of the Vice President and Ministry of Planning and National
Development, 1994). According to the Meru District Development
Plan, Tharaka Nithi District was carved out of Meru District on
April 2, 1992, about nine months after the St. Kizito Crime.

Library of Congress Cataloging-in-Publication Data available

Steeves, H. Leslie.
    Gender violence and the press : the St. Kizito story / H. Leslie
Steeves.
        p.   cm. — (Monographs in international studies. Africa
series : no. 67.)
    Includes bibliographical references and index.
    ISBN 0-89680-195-0 (pbk. : alk. paper)
    1. Violence in the press—Kenya. 2. Women in the press—Kenya.
I. Title. II. Series.
PN5499.K45S74   1997
302.23'2'096762—dc21   96-51586
                                                              CIP

For Fekerte and Anna

Contents

Illustrations, *ix*

Preface, *xi*

1. Context of the St. Kizito Crime, *1*

Introduction, *1*

Mass Media and Gender Violence, *3*

Patriarchal and Feminist Ideologies of Rape, *10*

The Context of Gender Oppression in Kenya, *17*

2. Interpreting Press Accounts, *22*

Method, *22*

The Case, *29*

Journalistic Patterns and Biases, *34*

Nine Media Frames, *40*

3. Patriarchal Framing, *42*

Ignoring or Marginalizing Rape, *42*

Emphasizing Government-Source Explanations:
Indiscipline, "Plotters," Mismanagement, *48*

Emphasizing School Critic Explanations: Stress and 8-4-4, *53*

Reinforcing Ethnic Prejudices:
"The boys never meant any harm . . . ," *56*

Reinforcing Patriarchal Rape Myths, *63*

Identifying Surviving Victims, But Not Assailants, *68*

Suggesting Survivor-Assailant Equality via Labels, *78*

4. Feminist Framing, *84*

Showing Concern for Survivors, *84*

Feminist Resistance, *87*

5. Conclusions, *96*

Appendices, *103*

A. List of St. Kizito Stories Analyzed, *103*

B. "Another St. Kizito Shocker," by Alex Riithi, *117*

C. Feminist Voices: Story Samples, *125*

"An Example of Violence Against Women," by Oketch Kendo, *125*

"Letter from the Editor," by Hilary Ng'weno, *128*

"Ministry Should Act Promptly Over Children," by Mkanju, *129*

"Family Violence: Women's Bodies Take up the Cudgel,"
by Cecilia Kamau, *131*

"Rape: Why the Apathy," by Rasna Warah, *134*

"School Attack Inspires Action by Women of Kenya,"
by Michele Landsberg, *136*

"Rape: Violation of Woman's Rights," by Esther Kamweru, *139*

Notes, *145*

Bibliography, *177*

Index, *185*

Illustrations

Map of Kenya and Meru District, *xvi*

Illustration 1.
Sunday Nation feature, 21 June 1992, *30*

Illustration 2.
Daily Nation front page, 15 July 1991, *44*

Illustration 3.
Weekly Review cover, 19 July 1991, *69*

Illustration 4.
The Standard front page, 30 June 1991, *72*

Illustration 5.
Daily Nation front page, 17 June 1991, *102*

Preface

This study examines print media coverage of a crime[1] of gender violence that occurred at St. Kizito Mixed Secondary School in Meru District, Kenya in mid-July, 1991. Nineteen girls were murdered and over seventy were raped or gang-raped by their male colleagues at the school. At the time the crime occurred, I was living in Kenya and teaching at the School of Journalism, University of Nairobi. Like others in Kenya and elsewhere, I was stunned and devastated by the enormity of the event. I had many conversations with my Kenyan students and colleagues —both about the crime itself and the local news reports. I also was able to observe the initial public discussion firsthand, including the growing antiviolence activism of Kenyan women and their efforts to gain a voice in media.

During my remaining six weeks in Kenya, I read and saved all local press accounts related to St. Kizito, including letters and editorials. Upon my return to Oregon, I collected many stories from American newspapers as well. All of these stories remained in my files until the summer of 1993, when I began rereading them, and considering their lessons. In this process, I quickly realized that I needed stories beyond my stay in Kenya, and I obtained funding to gather the Kenyan stories for the full year following the crime. At the same time, I gathered additional international reports via the database LEXIS/NEXIS.

I am grateful, first, to the Fulbright-Hays program, which allowed me to teach in Nairobi for eight months in 1991. Without the Fulbright grant, this study would not have been carried out. Of my Nairobi colleagues who provided assistance or encouragement, I especially thank Absalom Mutere, Wambui Kiai, Wanjiku Kabira, Waithira Gikonyo, and Kwame Boafo. I also am grateful to my thirty-two University of Nairobi journalism students (class of 1991), with whom I recall many helpful conversations about gender relations in Kenya and about the St. Kizito crime. Some of the students carried out research projects on gender representations in the press, and their works are cited here.

In addition, I am indebted to the University of Oregon School of Journalism and Communication for much support, including approving the leave time necessary to do this research and providing research assistance. I thank University of Oregon students Jane Kabira, Anne Kavenaugh, and especially Nancy Worthington, who assisted with the first version of this monograph, presented to the Association for Women in Development convention in Washington, D.C., October 1993. This early version was revised slightly and presented to the Association for Education in Journalism and Mass Communication convention in Atlanta, Ga., August 1994.

The University of Oregon Center for the Study of Women in Society provided financial support for obtaining Kenyan newspaper accounts published following my stay in Kenya, including all stories, letters, and editorials that appeared through 30 July 1992. David Easterbrook, curator of the Melville J. Herskovits Library of African Studies, Northwestern University, was enormously helpful in my efforts to obtain these stories. Brett Shadle did the work of locating and photocopying the stories, and generously responded to my additional requests for information well beyond the duration of our agreement. Once these additional stories (and related materials) arrived in Oregon, Jason Roman helped catalogue and read them, and also carried out numerous time-consuming tasks up to the point of publication. His library, editorial and computer skills contributed significantly to the completion of this study. Others who graciously assisted with necessary prepublication tasks include Morompi Ole-Ronkei, Susan Walsh, Beate Gersch, Dan Britz, and Andrea Soule.

This manuscript's path to publication was an unusual one. Along the way I received invaluable guidance from John Soloski, editor of *Journalism and Mass Communication Monographs*. Anonymous reviewers of that journal also gave helpful feedback. Other academic colleagues who provided scholarly assistance include: Carolyn Stewart Dyer, who supplied important sources and interpretations on rape and rape reporting and read and commented on the manuscript meticulously; Jeff Land, who guided my efforts to understand and apply Gramsci's hegemony; and Cheris Kramarae, Wayne Wanta, and Timothy Njoora, who also read the manuscript and provided feedback.

I am very grateful to the staff of Ohio University Press for their support, encouragement, and technical assistance. Gillian Berchowitz's efforts were especially crucial for the publication of this monograph. I also thank the press—specifically, the *Daily Nation* (Nation Newspapers, Ltd.), *The Standard* (E. A. Standard), the *Kenya Times* (Kenya Times Media Trust, Ltd.), the *Weekly Review* (Stellascope, Ltd.), and the *Toronto Star* (Toronto Star Syndicate)—for allowing me to reprint selected stories and illustrations. All of these stories and illustrations add much to this volume. I am most grateful for the seven stories in Appendix C, highlighting some of the rare and important feminist voices in the St. Kizito narrative.

I cannot close my acknowledgments without thanking my

husband, Dan Reece, and my daughters, Fekerte Reece-Steeves and Anna Steeves-Reece. My daughters, especially, inspired this work. I did the research, in part, because I have daughters. They serve as reminders of the unspeakable suffering of the St. Kizito survivors and of the nineteen girls who died, as well as the grief and trauma suffered by their families.

Finally, while many people deserve acknowledgment and credit for the strengths of this study, I assume full responsibility for any errors or inconsistencies the book may contain.

Gender Violence
and the Press

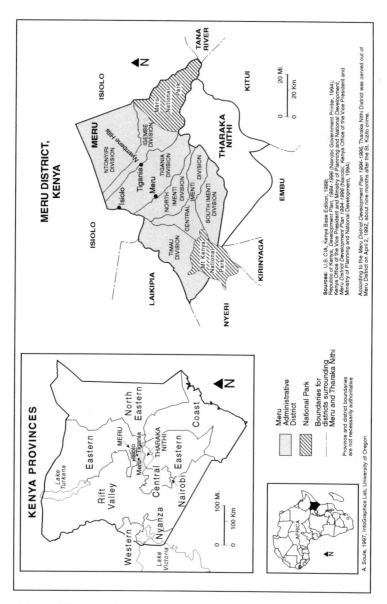

Maps of Kenya and Meru District

1

Context of the St. Kizito Crime

Introduction

On 13 July 1991, shortly before midnight, 306 boys attacked an overcrowded dormitory containing 271 girls at St. Kizito Mixed Secondary School in Meru District, Kenya, a rural area northeast of Nairobi. Nineteen girls suffocated or were crushed to death, more than seventy were raped or gang-raped, and many suffered additional injuries requiring hospitalization. Although many people lived close to the school and the police station was nearby, help did not arrive until nearly three hours after the incident. By then the assailants had disappeared into the dark and the victims lay bleeding and in shock amidst the dormitory ruins.

The crime took place during a time of considerable unrest in Kenyan secondary schools and universities. Riots and property destruction were common. Boys sometimes raped girls as well, with little media attention or public outrage. But because nineteen girls died and such a large number were raped, the St. Kizito incident shocked the nation and triggered unprecedented media and public discussion about gender violence and oppression.

This study analyzes Kenyan print media coverage of the crime with an emphasis on the following year—from the first day of coverage, 14 July 1991, through late July 1992. Every story, editorial, and letter about St. Kizito that appeared in three Kenyan daily newspapers and a weekly newsmagazine during that one-year time frame are included. In addition, I examined a sample of international reports from the database LEXIS/NEXIS.

The main focus of this study is the role of media in hegemonic process, that is, the process of securing consent for male-dominant (patriarchal) views while allowing some openings for challenges to these views. In the system of patriarchy, rape and rape-murder constitute the extreme of male force, violence, and domination. What, then, is the role of media in the dialectic between force and consent, domination and hegemony?[1] It is within this dialectic that this study is positioned.

The lessons of this study cannot be revealed except in their proper context, including prior scholarship on hegemonic process in mass media, media representations of gender, realities and myths about rape, Kenyan women's roles and status, and other contextual information on local politics and mass communication organizations. In light of this context, I located and read each story to determine whether and how patriarchal hegemony was revealed and reinforced. I also sought evidence of feminist perspectives.

In carrying out this analysis, I assume that the messages of mass communication contribute significantly to cultural ideology, that is, to shared values about what constitute appropriate attitudes and behaviors. I further assume that people with different ideological interests will struggle to gain a voice in the media, and that these interests can be detected via close readings of media content. It is important to acknowledge, however, that the *content* of communication constitutes just one facet of the *process* of communication. I am hopeful that this research will provide information and ideas helpful in other studies that carefully consider receivers and producers of the St. Kizito stories. Further, in the absence of systematic data from reporters and other gatekeepers, I note that my critique is of patterns of coverage, *not* of individual reporters. Most of the reporters who covered St. Kizito undoubtedly did the best they could, given their preparation and the constraints under which they worked.

This study joins others' efforts to describe news as hegemonic process, in this case, a process of patriarchy. Further, in extending scholarship on media representations of gender violence beyond the boundaries of industrialized societies, this study increases our knowledge of how media respond to gender violence and oppression. Finally, this study aims to contribute to global activism against gender violence by researching lessons to be learned from this crime, transmitting the findings, and encouraging further study of St. Kizito and crimes of gender violence in other global contexts.

Mass Media and Gender Violence

As noted above, this research assumes the significance of mass media as contributors to cultural ideology. Mass media, along with other ideological institutions (such as schools, churches, and families), help sustain societal values, and also are capable of challenging them. Critical communication scholars often draw on Louis Althusser to argue the importance of ideological institutions (such as those embedded in state apparatuses) in sustaining and reproducing social relations of production.[2]

Althusser describes society as made up of three kinds of processes and institutions: economic (involving production), ideological (involving representation), and political (involving social organization). These three are believed to be relatively autonomous, yet linked "by an unspoken web of ideological interconnections, so that the operation of any one of them is 'overdetermined' by its complex, invisible network of interrelationships with all the others."[3] Major change in one area will reverberate through the system.

Many critical scholars also draw on Antonio Gramsci's writings on hegemony, which go further than Althusser in specifying the processes of cultural rule through the structuring of ideology.[4] In Gramsci's view, ideologies "'organize' human masses, and create the terrain on which men [*sic*] move, acquire consciousness of their position, struggle, etc."[5] Hence, hegemony refers to an ongoing *process*, not merely to *ideas* imposed by the ruling class. It relies on the creation of ideological common ground, or a degree of collective consciousness. It is revealed in everyday life, including popular culture and what is assumed to be common sense. In essence, it is the process by which societies are led via the structuring and restructuring of ideology, involving both persuasion from above and consent from below. Hegemony is constantly formed and reformed by social practices.

Gramsci describes two processes by which a hegemonic class is able to "articulate the interests of subordinate (subaltern) groups to its own by means of ideological struggle."[6] He refers to these processes as "domination" and "intellectual and moral leadership."[7] In her excellent interpretive essay, however, Chantal Mouffe uses the terms "transformative hegemony" and "expansive hegemony," which I have borrowed in this volume. Transformative hegemony uses legal and political force to secure unification. Although the process may be gradual and nonviolent, the consent that is won is passive. A more pervasive and subtle type of hegemony, expansive hegemony, is exercised by intellectual and moral leaders to create active consensus.[8] In this latter process, dominant groups remain dominant by securing the active consent of subaltern classes. They do this by accommodating some of a subordinate group's interests but in a way that does not jeopardize dominant interests. For example, a policy may be implemented that supports the dominant ideology, while at the same time accommodating some interests of subordinate groups. In the case of media, the meaning of an event (e.g., a rape crime) may be reported to favor the dominant ideology while including some views of subordinate groups. "In other words, the dominant group is coordinated concretely with the general interests of subordinate groups, and the life of the State is conceived of as a continuous process of formation and superseding of unstable equilibria (on the juridical plane) between the interests of the fundamental group and those of the subordinate groups—equilibria in which the interests of the dominant group prevail, but only up to a certain point, i.e., stopping short of narrowly corporate economic interest."[9] This process also accounts for hegemonic *change*, in that expansive hegemony allows space within which subordinate groups may find ways to effectively challenge the symbols and cultural meanings that sustain a given cultural order. The process is one of articulation and rearticulation, wherein elements of an old system may be broken down and then rearticulated to meet a contradiction that has arisen in society, hence forming a system that can better accommodate the new situation.[10]

In that hegemony is grounded in people's everyday lives, mass media and popular culture constitute important battlegrounds for hegemonic struggle. Cultural studies scholars argue that mass media content is encoded to reinforce the dominant ideology, with certain meanings favored and other points of view excluded or de-emphasized. Those who draw on Gramsci seek to reveal how media function as agents of expansive hegemony by articulating interests of subaltern classes within the dominant view. This is done in many ways that usually are reinforced by media traditions and values, such as a present-time orientation, an emphasis on events versus issues, on individuals versus groups, on conflict, and on the unusual or sensational. Factors such as deadlines and economics also play a role.[11] Todd Gitlin's study of news coverage of the new left in the 1960s examines hegemonic process in part via the notion of "media frame," which refers to a pattern of selective emphasis and interpretation that—alongside news traditions and values (noted above)—naturalizes the world represented, in most cases the dominant ideology.[12] Gitlin's use of the framing concept was helpful in the research reported here, as will be discussed later.

One near-universal aspect of hegemony is gender inequality, as sustained by *patriarchy*, that is, processes and structures of male dominance. Feminists point out that the most powerful global and national institutions are owned and operated by men, and that their behaviors are not gender neutral. Although all feminists reject male dominance—or patriarchy—and seek change, they vary in how they analyze and challenge patriarchy. Classifications of the feminisms in terms of explanations that are biologistic (some forms of radical feminism), individualistic (liberal feminism) and/or sociocultural and economic (Marxist and socialist feminism) have remained in use, though they have been challenged by postmodernism and poststructuralism, which reject theoretical universalism.

Elsewhere I have advocated socialist feminism as a useful critical perspective that seeks to recognize diversity (by gender, race, class, and by other social divisions) while also locating conceptual and political common ground. Althusser's notions about economic, political, and ideological structures and processes have been influential in this perspective. The "economic" is addressed through the study of class oppression, which is considered a fundamental contributor to women's devaluation. The "political" is addressed in assessments of the patriarchal character of the state and the law. The "ideological" is examined via analyses of media, popular culture, and other ideological institutions that help perpetuate gender oppression.[13]

Many scholars influenced by socialist feminism now identify more with *feminist cultural studies*, which unites research and politics in efforts to identify and challenge expressions of hegemonic patriarchy in ideological structures and discourses.[14] Feminist cultural studies often draw upon Stuart Hall and others to assume that discourses are *polysemic*, that is, carry multiple and contradictory meanings, yet are encoded to carry preferred or dominant meanings for audiences. These varied meanings may be revealed via textual or discourse studies, studies that also examine historical context, recognizing that research and activism make sense only in light of historically understood conditions.[15]

Feminist scholars around the world have documented ways in which the products and processes of global media reflect patriarchal values—by ignoring and excluding women, by stereotyping women in narrow traditional roles, and by degrading women via representations of them as sex symbols or objects of abuse. News, including crime news, has been examined by many researchers who have discovered that very little news is by or about women, uses female sources, or examines issues of particular salience to women, such as child care, women's health, women's economic status, abortion, or gender violence. Moreover, even when these topics do make the news, most sources are male and stories are neither sensitive to women's needs nor reflect feminist viewpoints.[16]

Although little research has been published on women and media in Kenya, the existing evidence points to a pattern quite similar to that found elsewhere in the world. Wagaki Mwangi found that few (less than 10 percent) of the major newspaper stories relate to women, and that the dominant images of women are as victims, mothers, and athletes (female athletes are mostly foreign, not Kenyan). Victoria N. Goro and Sophie A. Muluka-Lutta examined television advertisements and found that two-thirds of the female characters are decorative sex objects, and the rest are in the traditional roles of wife and mother. Catherine Njeri Rugene studied humor columns in the Nairobi dailies and found that columnists routinely treat women as sex objects and objects of abuse. Anne Obura systematically examined representations of males and females in children's primary-school textbooks and found that males dominate in pictures and in the text and are involved in modern, technologically sophisticated activities, whereas females are almost always portrayed in traditional roles.[17]

Most studies of women and media tend to reflect liberal feminism's concern with individual achievement in the public sphere. As such, they assume that women's major problems in the media are too few representations, demeaning representations, and insufficient numbers of upper-level employees. When media content is examined, stereotypes of females are typically counted and classified, with relatively little analysis of their historical and contextual meanings. In contrast, critical scholars, including those who identify with feminist cultural studies, undertake historically-grounded analyses of ideological structures and processes, showing how these processes reflect and contribute to mutually reinforcing forms of oppression. In the context of Kenya, Nancy Worthington's in-depth analysis of two feature stories in Nairobi's *Daily Nation* reveals a variety of ways in which the text reinforces both indigenous and colonial forms of gender oppression, as well as class divisions between elite and poor women. Elsewhere, critical scholars have applied hegemony theory to media entertainment. Bonnie Dow's study of the *Mary Tyler Moore Show* and Shuchiao Yang's study of a woman's magazine in Taiwan, for instance, focus on patriarchal hegemony, arguing that hegemony incorporates small amounts of feminism in order to protect the dominant patriarchal ideology from change.[18]

Some feminists recently have examined mass media's role in marginalizing reports of gender violence and in perpetuating myths. Consider, for instance, the last sentence of a *New York Times* story released following Iraq's invasion of Kuwait in August of 1990: "To this point, no Americans have been reported harmed, although some who have escaped Iraq and Kuwait say that some non-American foreign women have been raped by Iraqi troops."[19] The reassurance that "Americans" have not been harmed is consistent with U.S. news values, which usually prioritize Americans (and "first world" citizens believed most closely alligned with Americans, e.g., Europeans), and de-emphasize harm to others. The redundant delineation of "non-American foreign women" as the only victims may be read as further reassurance that no one of significance has suffered. The fact that this excerpt is the last sentence in the 1048-word story means that rape is not considered particularly important information; moreover, the sentence was likely dropped from many newspapers that picked up the story. In general, then, this report implies that rape—especially wartime rape with non-American victims[20] —is not newsworthy information for the U.S. press. This is consistent with rape myths that deny or diminish the extreme harm that rape victims experience.

Based on the assumption that media have the power to reinforce rape myths or challenge these myths, Helen Benedict examined the media coverage of four highly publicized rape crimes in the United States, each involving one female victim. One was a case of marital rape, one a case of acquaintance rape, and two were gang rapes. She found that journalistic values and constraints, previously noted, interacted with rape myths and with reporter biases and prejudices to produce stories that were not only misleading and inaccurate, but likely increased the suffering of victims. Several other studies of how media cover violence against women have reported consistent findings: that media coverage reinforces patriarchal conceptions of rape and other forms of gender violence.[21]

A study particularly salient to this research is Elizabeth Farstad's analysis of news coverage of the New Bedford rape case. Farstad asked which of three ideologies of rape—liberal feminist, socialist feminist, or patriarchal—achieved hegemony in how newspapers covered this case. As anticipated, she found that the patriarchal ideology dominated, though liberal and socialist feminist perspectives gained some space.[22]

Little research thus far has considered media coverage of gender violence outside of the industrialized world. Yet global coalition-building can be supported by studies revealing cross-cultural similarities and differences in accounts of gender violence. The magnitude of the St. Kizito crime, plus its relative neglect globally, indicates an especially urgent need for research examining the event, including its media coverage.[23]

Patriarchal and Feminist Ideologies of Rape

An examination of the St. Kizito stories requires knowledge of what is known about patriarchal and feminist ideologies of rape. While patriarchal ideology claims to condemn rape, it legitimizes rape by endorsing myths that view it as "normal" under some circumstances. Patriarchal ideology is grounded in patriarchal notions of male and female sexuality, that is, the notions that males are innately aggressive and females are innately submissive and receptive. Men's overwhelming sex drive is "kept in check only by fear of the law and by respect of women's 'honor.'" "Honor" refers to a woman's virginity or her sexual loyalty to her husband. But the law may be insufficient, "as in time of war, at night, or in secluded places, or there may be an excuse to disregard a woman's 'honor,'" for instance, if a man perceives a woman as somehow "asking for it" by her dress or personal history. Hence, in patriarchal ideology, rape is wrong when it violates what rightfully belongs to men: women's virginity or sexual fidelity, depending on marital status. The focus is on what the victim of rape may have done to invite rape, not the rapist's responsibility for the crime.[24]

Feminists reject patriarchal ideology that excuses rape under certain circumstances. However, they vary somewhat in their analysis and their approach to change. For instance, liberal feminism yields a focus on how rape and the fear of rape thwart women's ability to participate equally with men in public life. The solution is to change discriminatory rape laws and practices, create new, more effective laws, plus strengthen deterrents against and punishments for rape. Much antiviolence activism therefore indicates a liberal feminist emphasis.

At the international level, feminists have pursued two major lines of argument. First, they have argued that freedom from gender violence is an international human right, one that must be explicitly addressed in human rights conferences and resulting documents and actions. At the June 1993 United Nations Human Rights Conference in Vienna, the Institute for Women, Law, and Development organized the Workshop on Gender and Human Rights. In addition, women's presence and activism at that conference resulted in the recognition of gender abuse and violence as human rights violations in the Declaration of Vienna and Program of Action. (However, the structures for implementing the recommendations have not been mandated.) Second, feminists have argued that gender violence is a major obstacle to economic development. This argument builds on considerable evidence that sustainable development is impossible until women are full participants in the process. Yet how can women participate while remaining oppressed by widespread violence and the fear of violence? The United Nations Development Fund for Women (UNIFEM) has played a leadership role in making arguments about gender violence as an obstacle to development, as well as in gathering global statistics on gender violence.[25]

Both of the above arguments were emphasized in discussions at the United Nations Fourth World Conference on Women, held in Beijing in September of 1995, where violence against women was one of twelve critical areas of concern. To address this problem, the Beijing Declaration and Platform for Action encouraged a number of actions: continued research on root causes; the creation of national laws consistent with the declaration; new training programs for law enforcement and health workers; increasing the participation of women in law enforcement and judicial professions; providing increased legal and social assistance to victims; adopting measures to protect particularly vulnerable girls and women; and taking action against sex trafficking and forced prostitution.[26]

In more local contexts, many national and community organizations have struggled to document and educate the public about gender violence. They also have devised and implemented strategies to revise pertinent laws and policies, raise public awareness and knowledge, assist victims, deter perpetrators, and generally increase the safety of women and girls.[27]

Nearly all feminists endorse and participate in liberal activism, but those with a more critical orientation note that the prevalence and experience of gender violence, including rape, vary by economic class, race, nation, and other historic social divisions. Hence, they view rape as enmeshed with complex problems of male dominance and oppression in society. In essence, feminist critical and cultural studies view rape as a part of patriarchal hegemony, which is profoundly related to capitalist hegemony, white hegemony, and so forth—depending on context. Therefore, the solution to rape requires more than changing and strengthening laws and policies. It also requires understanding and intervening in the complexities of all areas of society, including processes and structures of ideology, politics, and economics.[28]

Research supports a critical emphasis on historical context and on the complex intersections among many forms of oppression. Although cross-cultural studies—for example, those by Peggy Reeves Sanday and David Levinson—show that gender violence, including rape, occurs to some extent in nearly every society, there appears to be less gender violence in societies where women participate in the public sphere, men are involved in family life, and the surrounding culture condemns interpersonal violence. Rape incidents are greater in societies where men express contempt for women's public-sphere participation, where men have little or no role in child rearing, and where interpersonal violence is encouraged as an expression of masculinity. [29]

In every social context, rape is both perpetrated and experienced as an act of violence where sex is used as a weapon. The overwhelming majority of rapes are committed by males against females. Most rapes involve assailants and victims of the same race, ethnicity, and class, in contrast to a widespread American myth that non-whites rape whites. Another common myth is that rapists are insane, yet studies have shown that both stranger and acquaintance rapists are usually not insane, and are responsible for their behaviors.[30]

The most damaging and pervasive myth about rape is that it is motivated by lust, hence the related myths that women provoke rape (by their looks or behaviors) and that modest women are not raped. In reality, the rapist's goal is not sex and his motivation is not lust, but the domination, degradation and humiliation of the victim. His motivations are usually *anger* and *control*. The victim's experience is one of torture, but an especially extreme form, because her most intimate space is invaded and defiled. This experience is greatly magnified in gang rape.

> To be attacked by a rapist in any situation is a horrifying and humiliating experience. In most cases, the victim's fear of being killed is uppermost in her mind and emotions. To be confronted by a gang of rapists is even worse—one of the most terrible experiences human beings can inflict on another person. The victim's realization of helplessness becomes total, for if she is very nearly powerless against a single rapist, she is almost always a complete prisoner of a group. Her fear of death, torture, mutilation, and pain at the hands of many men is doubled and redoubled. . . . Group rape is the epitome of sexual sadism.[31]

Studies in the United States show that group rape, defined as multiple assailants against one victim, account for about one-third of all reported rapes and three-quarters of rapists. Yet relatively little research has examined group-rape behavior. Comparative studies indicate that the level of aggression is greater in group rape than in solitary rape, that group rapists are more likely to use alcohol or drugs, and that they are more likely to plan attacks. In addition, group rapists tend to be younger than solitary rapists, sometimes adolescents or college students, as in fraternity gang rapes. Despite the greater aggression in group rape and the extreme suffering of victims, group rape is harder to convict than solitary rape, and fewer cases make it to court. One factor is the typical youth of perpetrators, hence the attitude that "boys will be boys," and that their behaviors constitute outgrowable "antics of adolescent sexual exuberance." On the other hand, if grown men are involved (in group or solitary rape), the victim usually is blamed, with the assumption that she wanted it or deserved it.[32]

A common myth in group rape is that only certain individuals are responsible, not the whole group. Most experts, however, assert it is the *group* that rapes. The group does typically have a leader or leaders who plan the attack, but once the attack is underway it operates according to well-studied principles of collective or mob behavior, where all participate and group dynamics submerge the moral objections of individuals. The bond that holds group members together is their shared understanding of their sexuality, including women's place relative to men. Hence, the group rape has been hypothesized to be a "microcosm" of the larger patriarchal society.

> The cultural context of group rape is a society based on male-dominant authority structure. In such a system, fraternal (i.e., male) interests are justified and solidified through institutionalization. . . . This androcentric pattern is simply reiterated within the group rape situation. The victim is not the subject but the object of the situation. What is important is the maintenance of the male relational system—the shared sense of maleness—and the resultant feeling of power over femaleness, in self and others. The corollary to such a relational system is the overt cultural acceptability of rape in general and group rape in particular.[33]

Rozee-Koker and Polk found evidence for this theory in a

survey of a police department, an institution chosen because it is male-dominated and particularly salient in rape cases. They found correlations between inaccurate knowledge of group rape, male-stereotyped traits, and beliefs about the normalcy of rape. Also, many officers indicated more tolerant attitudes toward group than individual rapists, and the authors expressed concern that this tolerance may have serious implications if it indicates identification with the group rapist.[34] Given that newspapers also are male-dominated institutions with an involvement in rape crimes, a similar concern may apply; that is, institutional male bonding may increase the likelihood that hegemonic patriarchy is reinforced in media practice.

The scholarship on gang rape cited thus far is based on data gathered in the United States. To the extent, however, that nearly all societies are patriarchal and that violence against women is global, it is likely that many of the patterns revealed in this research appear elsewhere. In fact, many aspects of the St. Kizito crime are consistent with the above research on gang rape. The St. Kizito offenders (and victims) were young, most between ages of 14 and 18. Offenders and victims were of the same race, class, and ethnicity. Alcohol or drugs were involved. The crime was planned, and there were leaders. The courts were lenient on perpetrators. St. Kizito stands out from most group rapes primarily in the extremely large number of offenders and victims and the nineteen concurrent murders.

This study assumes, based on Sanday's and Levinson's research, that the likelihood and nature of rape crimes in a society depend in part on historical context in relation to gender roles and interpersonal violence.[35] The context of gender oppression and violence in Kenya is therefore significant in an analysis of media coverage. Later, in chapter 2, I will consider gender relations more locally in Meru District.

The Context of Gender Violence in Kenya

Most Kenyan women (about 87 percent) live in rural areas. As elsewhere in sub-Saharan Africa, Kenyan women have vital economic and social roles. Kenyan women are responsible for at least 75 to 80 percent of the farm labor, as well as for the bearing, rearing, and nurturing of the next generation. Many women additionally sell goods in the informal market. Despite these vital contributions, women do not benefit fairly from their labor. Many studies have shown that cash profits, extension services, new technologies, and financial credit are directed primarily toward men.[36]

In addition, most women do not receive equal access to education. Yet women's education, in particular, shows significant correlations with positive societal change. In Kenya, primary-school attendance by boys and girls is now almost equal, though more girls drop out before reaching secondary school. Women who do manage to advance in school often experience much discrimination and harassment. Once they graduate, the discrimination continues, as indicated by data showing many more employed men than women and almost no women in higher paying and managerial occupations. In addition, women have been all but absent from governmental policy-making roles.[37]

Explanations for women's oppression in Kenya are complex and must consider precolonial gender roles—including indigenous forms of patriarchy, colonial patriarchy (and accompanying notions about women and the private sphere), and the continued influence of Western economic, political, and religious (primarily Christian) values. In the realm of communication, for instance, precolonial African women had powerful roles as storytellers, information resources, and keepers of particular traditions and rituals. While men may have wielded greater power in some areas of overlap between women and men, women's roles were significant and revered. The introduction of colonial and postcolonial media and communication organizations (newspapers, television stations, extension communication systems, religious organizations, etc.) weakened women's informational roles, by giving control of these new and increasingly powerful organizations to men.[38]

Alongside the above historic factors, tensions among ethnic groups may act to further disadvantage and silence women. All of these complexities are illustrated in Patricia Stamp's analysis of the legal struggle of a Kikuyu widow, Wambui Otieno, to bury her Luo husband, S. M. Otieno, in Nairobi, where the two had lived and raised a large family. Common law supported a Nairobi burial, while customary (that is, traditional Luo) law stipulated a burial at S. M. Otieno's rural birthplace. Wambui was fought and ultimately defeated by his clan's determination to bury her husband at his rural birthplace. In her analysis, Stamp reveals a "collaborative hegemony" between political structures and processes within the state to control gender relations.[39] Despite the workings of hegemony, Stamp argues persuasively that Wambui's struggle opened political space for women, and showed that women need not be passive recipients of oppressive policies. "Moreover, Wambui showed Kenyan women the possibility of defiance. Not many would wish to be defamed as she was, but she proved that women could resist the control of their marital lineage and use the courts to do so. Wambui thus opened the political space for women's actions and, in this sense, she won."[40]

Kenyan women's traditional strengths, their organizations, and the efforts of individual, courageous women like Wambui Otieno deserve credit for the extent to which women today are considered at all in public policy. However, some activists feel that Kenyan women have not yet fought hard enough and note that the dominant women's organizations have been co-opted and controlled by men.[41] Regardless of one's analysis, the fact remains that postcolonial Kenyan women's organizations have wielded little political power and have had little voice, even on issues of obvious and crucial concern to women.

One major issue is violence against women and girls, which remains widespread in Kenya. Although gender violence in the form of child abuse and incest, female genital mutilation, domestic violence, and rape are illegal in Kenya, many people accept women's inferior status, including a silent tolerance of violence. Battered women may not resist, fearing further violence if their husbands stay or economic loss if they leave. Many people witness or experience gender violence but do not speak out because of societal beliefs about women's inferiority. In addition, rape by police and other security personnel is a widespread problem, well-documented by Amnesty International, and contributes to women's reticence to report rape.[42]

Kenyan law, derived from British common law, defines rape as follows: "Any person who has carnal knowledge of a woman or girl without her consent or with her consent if the consent is obtained by force or by means of threats or by intimidation of any kind, or by bodily harm or by means of false representations as to the nature of the act, or in the case of married women, by impersonating her husband is guilty of a felony termed rape."[43] The stated penalty for raping or attempting to rape an adult is imprisonment with hard labor for life with or without corporal punishment. Ironically, the stated penalty for rape of a child under fourteen years (the lowest age at which consent can be lawfully obtained) is less severe: imprisonment with hard labor for fourteen years with corporal punishment.[44]

Despite the relative clarity of the law, the actual practice of identifying rape or sentencing perpetrators has not been clear or consistent. Kenyan women activists have argued that Kenya's male-dominated courts have inadvertently encouraged rape via a reluctance to convict assailants and the general leniency of sentencing. Up to the time of the St. Kizito crime, there had been no recorded instance of a convicted rapist sentenced to the maximum penalty, with most sentences rarely more than three years. Also, whatever the facts of the case, victims usually are required to prove they did not consent to a sexual act or that "the consent was obtained by means of force, threats, intimidation, fear of actual bodily harm or false representation." This expectation, plus frequent difficulties in obtaining forensic evidence (i.e., the presence of semen and/or of bruises or lacerations on the woman's vagina) make a court appearance an intimidating decision for victims and increase the difficulty of convicting accused assailants.[45]

The prevalence of gender violence and oppression in Kenya is undoubtedly sustained by a complex web of hegemonic, patriarchal processes. This study argues that mass media reinforce patriarchy by contributing to a climate where it is acceptable to support women only in a narrow range of traditional and oppressive roles and where gender violence is tolerated or encouraged. In addition, media constitute an important site for ideological struggle and change. Although media are not the only ideological apparatuses of gender oppression, they do constitute a vital factor, one that is becoming more significant with the expansion of communication technologies.

The magnitude of the St. Kizito crime and its role as a catalyst for feminist activism point to its value as a case study, in this instance, a study of the patriarchal process of news. The enormous media attention given this crime seems at first a contradiction within hegemony, in that it acknowledges the reality of gender violence. This study seeks to examine the nature of this coverage and whether and how patriarchal hegemony was challenged or reinforced. The general research questions that guide the analysis are: In what ways did media reinforce patriarchal hegemony in reporting the crime and in representing victims and assailants? When and to what extent did feminist perspectives gain a voice in media?

2

Interpreting Press Accounts

Method

The methodology utilized in the preparation of this volume was a qualitative textual analysis, emphasizing an in-depth reading of stories about St. Kizito. Further, the study was not merely *qualitative*, but also *interpretive*. Liesbet van Zoonen argues that while interpretive research is usually qualitative, interpretation better captures the work of feminist and critical scholars, for example, by emphasizing some degree of first-hand involvement and an explicit political perspective. Interpretive textual analysis is appropriate in this study because of my interest in encoded meanings as indicated in a complex interplay among news traditions and constraints, uses of language, story placement, sources selected, and information emphasized or marginalized, alongside my feminist political stance. In essence, the research investigated how a variety of practices and decisions framed the crime, and whether this framing served to reinforce or challenge patriarchy. Hence, the analysis did not lend itself to standard criteria for quantitative content analysis, such as mutual exclusivity between categories or statistical reliability.[1]

The sample for this study was a *census*. It is usually recommended that qualitative researchers examine *all* relevant data because their interest in entwined and evolving social meanings does not fit with assumptions about the random scattering of discourse. The study includes every story that mentioned the St. Kizito incident (including letters and editorials) that appeared in the three Nairobi daily newspapers (plus their Sunday "sister" papers), as well as stories in a popular Nairobi-based newsmagazine, The *Weekly Review*, for the entire year following the crime: from 14 July 1991 though late July 1992 (to include all anniversary stories). In addition to the local stories, international press reports of the incident for the subsequent year were obtained via the database LEXIS/ NEXIS. In total, 339 stories about St. Kizito were identified and analyzed for the year following the crime. Also, many related stories on gender oppression and violence published that year were examined. To track more recent events in Kenya and globally, The *Daily Nation* and international reports were monitored through August 1994.[2]

The *Daily Nation* and *Sunday Nation*, published in Kiswahili and in English, are owned by the Prince Aga Kahn and have by far the largest national circulations of the Nairobi dailies. *The Standard* and *Sunday Standard*, owned until August 1995 by the London-based Lonrho Corporation, have the second largest circulation. The *Kenya Times* and *Sunday Times*, controlled and owned by the ruling political party, the Kenya African National Union, KANU, have the smallest circulation of the three. These publications constitute the daily news sources for most urban Kenyans and rely primarily on urban sources. Therefore their content is clearly urban-biased, a problem in African contexts, where most of the people live in rural areas. The urban bias is compounded by the papers' influence on government decision-makers, who read them daily, and on broadcast media, which rely on them or the urban sources they cite.[3] In addition, Nairobi print media often have a significant impact on international media, which have little access to primary sources and therefore quote them freely when convenient.

As indicated above, the study focuses entirely on press coverage, and does not consider television or radio stories. Although television is a significant factor for many major events, in this case it was not. Local and international television stories of St. Kizito were very few compared to press stories, and reached relatively few people. Local radio coverage was undoubtedly a significant source of information about the crime for rural Kenyans, but its content is unretrievable. In addition, I noted that most radio reports certainly were taken from print media.

Interpretation of the stories began with "a long preliminary soak" in the material, as advised by Stuart Hall for both quantitative and qualitative content analysis. In the case of quantitative content analysis the purpose of this "soak" is to develop valid coding categories. In qualitative analysis the goal is rather to identify valid themes and illuminating examples consistent with a conceptual argument or question.[4] In this research, upon locating the stories, I read them over and over again, taking notes each time. The fact that I was living in Kenya when the crime occurred and was able to observe the initial public discussion firsthand increased my contextual familiarity with the stories. In addition, this study required background research in relevant contextual areas (reviewed in chapter 1 and elsewhere).

My analysis is guided by Todd Gitlin's method of framing, which he adapted from prior scholarship[5] and used to reveal hegemonic process in the *New York Times* and CBS News television coverage of the anti-Vietnam War resistance movement, Students for a Democratic Society (sps), in the 1960s. Gitlin drew on his personal involvement in and knowledge of the movement and also immersed himself in the material, seeking media frames, which he defines as follows: "*Media* frames, largely unspoken and unacknowledged, organize the world both for journalists who report it and, in some important degree, for us who rely on their reports. *Media frames are persistent patterns of cognition, interpretation, and presentation, of selection, emphasis, and exclusion, by which symbol handlers routinely organize discourse, whether verbal or visual* (emphasis in original)."[6]

Framing devices that Gitlin identifies for news about the resistance movement include, for instance, trivialization (making light of movement behaviors), polarization (emphasizing counter-demonstrations), marginalization (showing demonstrators as deviants), disparagement by numbers (undercounting), overemphasizing right-wing opposition to the movement, and relying extensively on statements by government officials.[7] These and other framing devices were strengthened by media traditions such as focusing on events versus context, on conflict versus consensus, and on individuals versus groups. Other reinforcing factors include economic criteria, news deadlines, and journalists' ambitions. Gitlin demonstrates that, although the resistance movement did gain space in media, a variety of frames served to disparage the movement and reinforce the hegemonic economic and political interests of the news organizations.

Although neither Benedict's nor Farstad's studies of news coverage of rape discuss media framing, both studies use qualitative approaches consistent with framing, identifying biasing devices that are reinforced by news traditions and could be described as media frames. Both studies reveal considerable evidence of patriarchal hegemony as opposed to feminist points of view. Patriarchal hegemony is indicated in part via "fram-

ing devices," that is, marginalizing key facts, disproportion-
ately showing concern for criminals versus victims, ground-
ing explanations in social problems other than gender
oppression, and emphasizing themes and information consistent with rape myths, including myths involving intersections
of gender, race, and class.[8]

In reading stories about the St. Kizito crime, framing patterns were sought that would serve to reinforce hegemonic
patriarchy or to challenge patriarchy. Frames were identified
as I read and analyzed the stories. In other words, frames
came primarily from the St. Kizito stories, not from previous
research. Yet my contextual knowledge and related research
certainly supplied clues. For instance, as in Benedict's research, I read the stories seeking ways in which the press may
have reinforced patriarchy by deflecting attention away from
the crime and criminals, supporting rape myths, and/or
neglecting to show concern for victims or relay feminist perspectives. Also sought were indications of challenges to patriarchy, that is, showing concern for victims or exposing the
larger context of gender violence. Each story was read seeking which (and whose) of those issues raised by the incident
the press chose to emphasize, which issues were ignored and
how these issues supported patriarchal or feminist perspectives. Portrayals of victims and assailants also were examined,
including whether and when they were named and the labels
used to describe them. A further consideration was how pre-
dominant attitudes about gender roles and intersecting variables (e.g., religion and ethnicity), as well as how certain
newsroom practices may have supported the use of certain
framing techniques.

The following quantitative information was systematically
recorded in addition to the qualitative analysis: each story's
date, placement (page on which the story began), the gender of
the reporter, and the identification of assailants or victims via

names or photographs. For the first six weeks after the crime, labels used to describe assailants and victims were recorded, as well as length of stories (column inches) for the Kenyan stories.[9] These simple quantification procedures helped to organize the analysis, reveal certain patterns of coverage, and support some areas of the qualitative interpretation.

As acknowledged elsewhere, this study does have certain limitations characteristic of all examinations of communication content. It lacks systematic information gathered from Kenyan audiences of the St. Kizito stories—especially those with a primary interest in the coverage, including Meru area residents, Kenyan politicians, educators, leaders of women's organizations, and all women and girls. Nor does this study systematically tap the views or experiences of the reporters, editors, or other gatekeepers responsible for media coverage. Both types of data could extend, deepen, and support or contradict my interpretations. I encourage others to carry out these analyses.

The fact that I am not a Kenyan may additionally suggest an *etic* versus *emic* question frequently discussed in anthropology, that is, the question of whose values guide (and bias) the research: the values of the researcher or of the culture observed? In this study I sought evidence of support for patriarchy versus feminism in the news stories based on my reading of the stories and my knowledge of relevant literature and context. I believe that my experience of living in Kenya and my many conversations with Kenyans both in Nairobi and in Oregon were helpful in strengthening the cultural validity of this research. In addition, given the universality of gender prejudice and rape myths, most persons aware of these prejudices and myths are capable of seeing certain blatant manifestations wherever they occur. Also pertinent is the influence of Western news values on media around the world. Most Kenyan journalists (or their teachers) receive their training in

North America or Europe. Therefore, their traditions and values (e.g., related to sensationalism, connecting stories to ongoing news agendas, and emphasizing events versus context), which are potentially news-distorting, are much the same as those with which Americans and Europeans are familiar.[10]

The results are presented in narrative form, following an overview of the case and a discussion of patterns of media coverage in light of journalistic traditions and constraints. The narrative conforms roughly (not entirely) to time, beginning with early media frames and closing with feminist interventions. Nine framing patterns have been identified from the analysis, seven of which serve primarily to reinforce the patriarchal hegemonic view of rape (and other facets of hegemony at the time), and two of which challenge this view.

These nine frames overlap and evolve over time. They often are mutually reinforcing. They also intersect with media traditions and conventions in a mutually reinforcing manner. They are *not* mutually exclusive. Also, I do not claim that these are the only framing techniques used or that another researcher would describe them in the same way. Most critical scholars acknowledge that their analyses are interpretive, and that interpretation is never complete and always contested. As van Zoonen argues, the researcher's task is to "find a balance between faithfully reconstructing the meanings, definitions and interpretations" that emerge from the research material and "an analytic and encompassing picture" that illuminates the process of meaning-making under study.[11]

The Case

An overview of the case—including the local context, prior events, the political climate, and the crime itself—is necessary before presenting my analysis of the media reports. The St.

Kizito crime occurred in Meru District, located northeast of Nairobi and one of eight districts that make up the Eastern Province of Kenya. The more precise location was near Tigania town, about 18 miles north of Meru town and about 125 miles northeast of Nairobi. Tigania town is in Tigania Division close to the Igembe Division boundary in the north-central part of the District. I note that the Tigania and Igembe peoples together constitute two of eight Meru subgroups "united by common history, culture, and social institutions." The Tigania and Igembe subgroups are considered particularly close culturally and are jointly referred to as the Nyambenes, also the name of a range of hills in the north-central part of the District (just northwest of Meru National Park).[12]

The primary economic activity in the Nyambene area is agriculture, especially tea, coffee and miraa, a tree valued in many parts of East Africa for its young twigs, which are chewed for their mild stimulatory effect. Traditionally in Meru, only elders were allowed to use miraa outside of ceremonial rituals. The more widespread use of miraa as social controls have weakened has been controversial. However, the health and social problems from miraa use per se likely have been less serious than those created by the abuse of stronger drugs, primarily alcohol, which may be purchased with miraa profits.[13]

The traditional Nyambene life cycle was divided into age-sets, with different social responsibilities expected of each age set. Paul Goldsmith describes eight progressive groups for males: infant/child; uncircumcized boy; circumcision candidate; warrior; junior elder; ruling elder; ritual elder; and the gerontocracy.[14] The age-grade system did not apply to girls in the same way, though clitoridectomy traditionally was a significant event, indicating the girl's eligibility for marriage, usually in her late teens.[15]

Illustration 1. Sunday Nation feature, 21 June 1992. "St. Kizito: A Kenyan nightmare that won't go away," by Ngugi wa Mbugua, pictures by Tony Mbugguss, pp. 8–9. Photos depict the dormitory "death chamber," which remained a court exhibit a year after the crime and the new St. Cyprian Boys High School sign *(left)*, the new headmaster Michael Mbogori *(middle)*, the school compound *(top right)*, and Nairobi psychologist Gladys Mwiti *(lower right)*.

Circumcision traditionally was the occasion for a major social celebration, as it marked the transition from childhood to adulthood (warriorhood in boys), usually between the ages of 15 and 20.[16] Permission for a boy to be circumcised was not automatic but rather earned based on criteria of endurance and self-control. "Respect for elders, for oneself, and for one's age-mates was also promoted."[17] Once circumcised, warriors were expected to adhere to a strict code of ethics, including a sexual code, where sex was reserved for marriage only and sexual transgressions—including adultery, rape, sexual harassment and molestation—resulted in punishments such as severe beatings and large fines.[18] Girls also were expected to confine sex to marriage, and to practice norms of sex segregation, especially surrounding rituals for important occasions such as clitoridectomy, the circumcision of boys, and childbirth.[19]

The above description, emphasizing respect, self-control and sexual temperance in traditional Meru society, contrasts sharply both with the St. Kizito crime and the group's popular reputation (discussed in chapter 3) as "hot-headed" and "unpredictably violent."[20] The contrast certainly raises historical and anthropological questions about the gendered evolution of Meru age-set traditions and social controls, questions that deserve systematic and comparative study. Goldsmith notes that thus far the Meru group's violent reputation has *not* been substantiated by comparative statistics.[21]

In the larger context of Kenyan society, violence in schools certainly was widespread at the time of the St. Kizito crime. In prior months there had been much student unrest in many parts of the country, both in secondary schools and in universities. In secondary schools, the outcomes included extensive property destruction, with rapes and other injuries reported in some instances. Precipitating causes of this unrest, as reported by students, include complaints and anger about food, rules, fee increases (without adequate explanation), and perceived financial mismanagement and corruption. Most would agree, however, that these complaints masked deeper concerns about many problems, including inadequate facilities, overcrowding, financial difficulties, and increased academic demands due to the new "8-4-4" system of education. (The "8-4-4" is an American-style system with eight years of primary school, four years of secondary school, and four years of university. It had replaced a British-style system with thirteen years of pre-university education and three years in the university.) In some instances ethnic disputes were involved in the atmosphere of student unrest in Kenya.

In addition, frustrations related to general dissatisfaction with KANU, the ruling party, cannot be overlooked. The St. Kizito crime took place several months before a decision to allow multiparty politics was announced in December 1991. At the time of the incident there was widespread public frustration and distrust of government, but few outlets for venting the frustration. Censorship and self-censorship were widespread, and many journalists had been jailed for writing stories contrary to government views.

The precise facts of the St. Kizito crime probably never will be known and are not the primary focus of this volume. However, the following account, distilled from multiple reports, represents general agreement about what happened. St. Kizito Mixed Secondary School in Meru District was started in 1968 as a boys' school, sponsored by the Roman Catholic Church, but with partial government administration and support. It was named after a teenaged Ugandan martyr who died for his faith in the nineteenth century. In 1975 the school became mixed due to an increased need to accommodate girls within the education system. Over the years the student population increased. By July 1991 the boys' dormitory, which was meant for around 120 students, housed more than 300.

The girls' dormitories were equally congested until 1989, when a new dormitory was built. The school experienced student strikes in 1986, 1987, and 1989. After the third strike, a new headmaster was appointed, Mr. James Laiboni.[22]

There were some signs of student unrest several weeks before the St. Kizito crime. However, the immediate triggers were the boys' discontent over several, seemingly minor issues: the headmaster's refusal to allow them to attend a sports event because of nonpayment of activity fees; the boys' demand that their "entertainment time" be shifted from Friday to Sunday; complaints about tuition; and demands to remove a kiosk (vending stand) operated by a former student (girl), who reportedly had been "paid off" by the teacher who made her pregnant.

On Saturday, 13 July, the 306 boys became angry at the 271 girls for refusing to join their plans to strike. Some of the boys were using alcohol and drugs. Sometime between 8 and 9 P.M., the boys cut off all electric power to the school compound, forcing the girls to retreat to their dormitories. After the boys began shouting threats and hurling stones, all 271 girls were led by their prefects (student leaders) to the new dormitory, designed for 120 girls, because it had the most secure locks. There, the girls crowded together for several hours. Shortly before midnight the 306 boys attacked the building, breaking the windows and pounding down the door with a large rock. In the ensuing attack nineteen girls were suffocated or trampled to death, and at least seventy-one survivors were raped or gang-raped.[23] Many survivors suffered additional injuries requiring hospital treatment.

No immediate efforts were made to help the victims. The three watchmen said they were helpless against the assailants, and no one in the nearby hospital or homes came to help. The police, located a short distance away (less than a fifteen-minute walk) were alerted by 1 A.M., but did not arrive until after 3 A.M. When help finally arrived, nineteen bodies were removed. Most of the over-eighty injured victims were taken to nearly Tigania Mission Hospital and several were taken to Meru District Hospital.

The boys were ordered to return to the school for screening within a week. After intensive screening, thirty-nine suspects were arrested. Thirty were charged with nineteen counts of manslaughter and two were charged with rape and attempted rape. The trials took place between December 1991 and May 1992. Four of the suspects were found guilty of manslaughter and sentenced to four years in jail each, and several others were placed on probation.[24] The St. Kizito watchmen were charged with failing to prevent a crime, but were released within a month. No police officers were charged with negligence, and no news stories investigated the inadequate response of the Meru police.

The survivors were transferred to nine different girls-only schools within two weeks of the crime. Most of the St. Kizito boys not charged with rape or manslaughter were distributed among more than twenty new schools within a little over two months of the crime, at least one of which was coeducational. St. Kizito was renamed St. Cyprian and converted to a boys-only school, with entirely new students. The surviving girls received little in the way of counseling, and a *Sunday Nation* feature indicated that their academic performance was poor during the year following the ordeal.[25]

Journalistic Patterns and Biases

The bulk of the local and international reports about St. Kizito appeared during the first few weeks, with little in the news and almost nothing on the front page for the remainder of the year following the crime (see tables 1 and 2).

Table 1
Gender of Reporter by Newspaper and Quarter

	1st Quarter			2nd Quarter			3rd Quarter			4th Quarter			Totals
	M	F	NA	M	F	NA	M	F	NA	M	F	NA	
Daily Nation	29	3	25	12	0	7	3	0	3	1	1	5	89
Sunday Nation	9	3	1	2	0	0	0	0	1	2	1	0	19
The Standard	31	3	20	5	0	3	1	0	3	1	0	2	69
Sunday Standard	4	0	3	0	0	1	0	0	0	0	1	1	10
Kenya Times	34	4	12	4	0	2	2	0	1	0	0	2	61
Sunday Times	3	1	3	1	0	0	0	0	0	0	0	0	8
Weekly Review	9	0	11	0	0	1	0	0	1	0	0	1	23
International Reports	10	4	37	0	1	1	0	0	6	1	0	0	60
	129	18	112	24	1	15	6	0	15	5	3	11	339

Table 2
Placement by Newspaper and Quarter

	1st Quarter		2nd Quarter		3rd Quarter		4th Quarter		
	Pg. 1	Other	Pg. 1	Other	Pg. 1	Other	Pg. 1	Other	
Daily Nation	13	44	0	19	1	5	1	6	89
Sunday Nation	1	12	0	2	0	1	0	3	19
The Standard	11	43	0	8	1	3	0	3	69
Sunday Standard	0	7	0	1	0	0	0	2	10
Kenya Times	15	35	0	6	1	2	0	2	61
Sunday Times	0	7	0	1	0	0	0	0	8
Weekly Review	2	18	0	1	0	1	0	1	23
	42	166	0	38	3	12	1	17	279

Note: In both tables the four quarters refer to the following dates, respectively: 14 July–13 October; 14 October–13 January; 14 January–13 April; 14 April–31 July (to include July anniversary stories). In table 1, "M," "F," "NA" refer to gender of authorship: male, female, or unknown. The "not apply" category was used conservatively to include all stories with no byline, or with a gender-neutral byline such as "*Nation* correspondent." In reality, it is likely that most, if not all, of these stories were written by men, given the dearth of female reporters at the papers. In table 2, international reports are omitted.

The enormous amount of coverage at the outset and drastic tapering off of information later is consistent with the present-time and event-orientation of news in general, including crime news. The extensive initial coverage certainly also related to the sensational nature of the crime, which could enhance newspaper sales. Many local stories in fact indicate that rape and other forms of gender violence and abuse had been common in society and in schools, but that St. Kizito got attention because nineteen girls died.[26]

The St. Kizito crime involved ordinary (not famous or wealthy) Kenyans of the same class and ethnicity, contrary to media's common tendency to highlight rape stories where famous or upper-class people are involved, or when blacks rape whites.[27] Yet, because the St. Kizito event was so extreme, it was initially of great interest to the local media. This interest died off by the end of August, with only a few stories buried in back pages of the papers. Even the hearings and trials did not generate much coverage, with only two front-page stories each in the *Daily Nation* and the *Kenya Times* and one in *The Standard* between August 1991 and the end of July 1992. One front-page story appeared in each paper on 19 February, 1992 reporting jail sentences for four of the convicted offenders.[28]

In contrast, it is worth pointing out that during the time that the St. Kizito offenders were being tried and sentenced, the trials of two Maasai Mara (National Game Reserve) wardens for the 1988 murder of British tourist Julie Ward also were going on. This four-and-a-half-month trial, which involved a white, foreign, upper-class victim and two Kenyan suspects, was given enormous amounts of media space, including many front-page stories.[29] Also, the Mike Tyson rape trial took place in the United States during this time and was likewise allocated much more space and prominence in the Kenyan Press than St. Kizito. Obviously, Mike Tyson is an

African-American athlete of considerable international fame. Yet the decision of Kenyan newspapers to give his trial priority over St. Kizito can only be understood in terms of the strength of media conventions in rape cases, even in highly dramatic cases, once the initial shock wears off.[30] The coverage of the St. Kizito crime, therefore, supports other studies, as well as casual observation, showing that rape crimes are considered newsworthy when they are highly unusual, or when famous or rich people are involved, especially when poor blacks are accused of raping upper-class whites.

An obvious question about the coverage pattern is whether there were differences among the local papers. During the first six weeks (14 July–31 August 1991), when the bulk of the coverage occurred, the three papers published a total of 163 stories: 61 by the *Daily Nation*, 53 by *The Standard*, and 49 by the *Kenya Times*. These numbers, however, do not correlate with the amount of space each paper devoted to the crime. The *Kenya Times* (and *Sunday Times*), the semiofficial government paper, devoted the most space by far to the story, with 1,044 column inches. *The Standard* (and *Sunday Standard*) had the least coverage, with a little over half the space of the *Kenya Times*: 599 column inches. The space allocated by the *Daily Nation* (and *Sunday Nation*) was in between, with 785 column inches.[31]

Why the great interest in this crime on the part of the *Kenya Times?* An explanation must consider the reputation of the editor-in-chief at the time, Philip Ochieng. Ochieng was known for his strong personality, deep convictions, and stubborn determination in areas of personal concern. With regard to press coverage, Ochieng had a penchant for fixating on certain issues or events that captured his interest, resulting in much space and prominence for the stories as well as great pressure on reporters doing the work.[32] In the case of the St.

Kizito coverage, Ochieng's other writings do indicate a concern about gender oppression, which may help explain his paper's interest in the incident. In a book published in 1992, Ochieng accuses free press advocates of further oppressing women by encouraging advertising for oppressive beauty products and practices. According to Ochieng,

> Women have been among the most oppressed groups ever since private property appeared in society and so their consciousness of self-respect and their faculty of choice have been and continue to be as low as those of other oppressed groups in general. And yet the "freer Press" never ceases to argue that to seek to make political inroads into this assault on the dignity of women, this commercializing on their bodily eminences [*sic*], is to interfere with "freedom." The license to oppress a certain section of society through means so subtle that the oppressed themselves are the ones who come eventually to invite such oppression—an old tool of external as well as internal colonialism—is what these ladies and gentlemen mean by "freedom of expression."[33]

Also, the fact that the *Kenya Times* is the government paper and the news about St. Kizito could be framed to fit government agendas (see chapter 3) may have influenced the amount of coverage this paper gave the incident. Certainly, editors' and reporters' idiosyncrasies and their political ties affect news decisions. These factors, alongside economic considerations, may bolster the sensationalism of stories. They may also increase the sloppiness and inaccuracy of stories. In addition, as will be shown later, amount of space allocated (in this case study) bears little relation to the overall accuracy—or the gender-sensitivity—of the reporting.

The majority of the St. Kizito stories have bylines, indicating that most of the local and international reporters who covered the crime were men (see table 1 and appendix A). Benedict points out that men usually cover rape crimes because crime reporters usually are men.[34] The situation is somewhat different in Kenya, as all newsworthy events in rural areas tend to get covered by the reporters assigned to those areas. However, nearly all such "bureau chiefs" are men, as are the vast majority of reporters, editors, and other gate-keepers.[35] Virtually all of the early stories about St. Kizito are written by men, most of their sources are male, and only a few of these stories discuss the larger context of gender oppression in society or indicate sensitivity to the suffering of the victims.

In general, the question of the impact of the reporter's gender on patriarchal framing is not simple, as studies around the world have failed to show correlations between gender of reporter and gender-sensitivity of story. Rather, reporter socialization in school and the newsroom has a greater impact on how stories are written. This is largely because not all women are feminists, and most women who do have feminist agendas eventually conform to organizational norms, or leave.[36] I believe more case-study research is needed on this question, as there are many examples of feminists and other activists who have found ways to make a difference in mainstream media.[37] Plus, common sense suggests that the increased presence of women (beyond tokenism) supports the development and expression of feminist consciousness. Studies are needed to critically examine just how and within what contexts particular women (and some men) around the world do make feminist interventions.

In the coverage of St. Kizito, while most of the stories are by men, a few women eventually contributed by writing features, opinion pieces, and letters, as well as reports of women's organizational meetings and a 13 August memorial service.[38] Later I will show that these few women writers played a significant role in gaining some voice for feminist perspectives.

Although their stories and perspectives seldom got on the front page, their efforts were significant in raising questions about injustices experienced by women in Kenyan society.

Nine Media Frames

The traditions and patterns discussed above supported a number of framing techniques that reinforce patriarchal hegemony. The first is the near-absence of rape or other aspects of gender violence in early accounts of the crime, which focus almost entirely on the deaths and on the events leading to the "tragedy," as it was frequently referred to in the press. The second and third frames, related to the first, involve quoting prominent sources who have had political agendas to promote and who used St. Kizito simultaneously to highlight their agendas and excuse the assailants' behaviors.[39] Government sources attributed the crime primarily to school indiscipline caused by administrative mismanagement. Other obvious "expert" sources—primarily psychologists and educators—attributed the crime to academic stress from the previously noted changeover to the 8-4-4 system of education. The fourth frame serves to simultaneously excuse assailants and bolster existing ethnic prejudices by quoting local sources to describe gender violence as indigenous to the Meru ethnic group.

In addition to these frames, there is an inclination in news to make connections to widely accepted hegemonic myths. To the extent that patriarchal rape myths are accepted as part of common sense, it not surprising that news reports would include these myths in analyses. Two major myths—that rape is motivated by lust and that the victim is responsible—helped inspire many stories about the declining morality in youth and the failure of mixed-sex schools. The myth that group rape is perpetrated by a few individuals rather than the group is reflected in language use as well as widely reported efforts to catch the few assailants who were responsible. Additional frames that serve to support patriarchy include the identification of victims but not assailants, and the use of labels that equalize the status of assailants and victims.

Feminist resistance to patriarchy in media accounts gradually gained some space, though it was undermined by treatment and placement. This resistance includes efforts to show concern for the St. Kizito victims and to highlight feminist activism addressing specific types of gender violence and the larger context of gender violence and oppression.

3

Patriarchal Framing

Ignoring or Marginalizing Rape

The newspaper stories that appeared the first two days after the St. Kizito crime (Monday and Tuesday, 15 and 16 July 1991) were important in establishing the dominant (government) understanding of the incident, that is, that it was an example of gross indiscipline with tragic consequences. These consequences all but excluded mention of rape in the early accounts, especially in the *Daily Nation*, Kenya's most popular paper, where rape was rarely mentioned.

To an extent, this is understandable, in that murder is more serious than rape and the basic facts about who and how many died were known more quickly than the facts about the rapes. Yet information that multiple rapes had occurred was readily available via numerous eyewitness accounts. In addition, the basic fact that virtually *all* of the dead and injured victims were girls was obvious. Therefore the near-absence of the word rape in the first few days of coverage and the failure to consider seriously the gendered nature of the crime at the outset and in much subsequent reporting indicate consistency with hegemonic views that deny the seriousness of violence against women. The frequent use of the term "tragedy" supports this denial by suggesting blamelessness or forces beyond human control.

The page-one headline in the *Daily Nation* on 15 July 1991 is: "Moi orders Thorough Investigation as . . . Rampaging Boys Leave 19 Girls Dead" (second half in large type). Under the headline is a large photograph of unnamed female students sorting out their belongings in the "death chamber" where the crime took place. The *Nation* was the only local or international publication to run a photograph on 14 or 15 July. The story opens as follows: "Tragedy struck a mixed secondary school in Meru District when a boys' attempt to press girls into a strike against their headmaster left 19 girls dead and 67 injured." The remainder of the story quotes sources reporting on the conditions of injured girls, describing the incident, expressing shock, and suggesting motives. The sources include President Moi, who condemned "hooliganism" and "indiscipline" in schools. Other sources are Meru District hospital spokespeople, the school's headmaster, other school officials, and church officials. Of the eleven named sources, only one is female. She was a Form III victim, who spoke from her hospital bed about the motive for the crime: the girls' refusal to collaborate with the boys' strike plans. On the second page of the twenty-five-column-inch story there was one minor mention of possible rape with no named source: "The girls said that some of them were raped while others were trampled underfoot in the darkness."[1]

The headline of the 15 July *Kenya Times* story reads: "19 Girls Killed in School Rape" plus a very small subhead: "75 Girls Hurt in Attack by Boys." That is, in contrast to the *Daily Nation*, the fact of rape was noted at the outset in the *Kenya*

Illustration 2. Daily Nation front page, 15 July 1991. "Moi orders thorough investigation as . . . Rampaging boys leave 19 girls dead," by Irungi Ndirangu, Imanene Imathiu and KNA, picture by Joseph Odiyo. The photo caption is: "Death chamber . . . Students sort out their clothes strewn on the floor of their dormitory where rampaging boys left 19 girls dead and the room in a shambles."

Times report. However, here the identity of the assailants is not specified in the lead: "Nineteen schoolgirls at Kizito Secondary School, in Tigania, Meru District, died on Saturday night after they crowded into a dormitory to escape from boys who had attacked another dormitory and raped some girls." The story, by Alex Riithi, *Kenya Times* Meru correspondent and author of many subsequent St. Kizito stories, quotes hospital sources to indicate the girls' injury status. It also quotes a watchman to describe the sequence of events, which includes a statement that some girls "were raped and beaten up by the rioting boys," clearly St. Kizito boys (by the third paragraph). Toward the end of the nineteen-column-inch story President Moi is quoted, as in the *Daily Nation*, condemning "hooliganism and general indiscipline" in the schools. The story also notes an earlier incident at Kiriani Secondary School, where boys raped girls and destroyed property. [2]

The 15 July, nineteen-column-inch story in *The Standard* gives the most complete report of the crime. The headline refers to both victims and assailants and the facts of both death and rape: "Rampaging Students Flee after Incident . . . 19 Girls Killed in Rape Ordeal" (second half in large type). The specific location, hence identities of victims and assailants, are further detailed in the lead: "Nineteen girls at Saint Kizito mixed secondary school in Tigania Division of Meru District died after they were attacked and sexually assaulted by their male colleagues early yesterday." However, the lead gives the impression that only the 19 dead victims were raped. Following the lead, the story emphasizes President Moi's remarks condemning "indiscipline" and "hooliganism." Other sources quoted are: a police spokesman, describing the whereabouts of the boys; a hospital spokeswoman, describing the injury status of the victims and stating that many of those injured were raped; and two watchmen, who give an account of the incident. [3]

Initial international stories on LEXIS/NEXIS include brief 14 July Reuters and Agence France Presse (AFP) accounts of the incident, longer AFP and Reuters accounts on 15 July and brief acounts in *Newsday*, the *New York Times*, the *Washington Times*, the *St. Petersburg Times*, *USA Today*, the *Orlando Sentinel Tribune*, and the *Chicago Tribune* on 15 July. All of these accounts (except one 15 July Reuters story, by Manoah Esipisu) rely entirely on Kenyan newspaper accounts or stories issued by the government-operated Kenya News Agency (KNA). Even the *New York Times* story comes from Reuters text, which in turn was taken from KNA accounts. Most of these stories do note the fact that rapes occurred. It is worth pointing out, however, that of the headlines accompanying these stories, only the *Washington Times* and *New York Times* headlines name the St. Kizito boys as the assailants: "Boys Raid Girls' Dorm; Many Raped, 19 Die," (*WT*); "Boys at Kenya School Rape Girls, Killing 19" (*NYT*). The other headlines use the passive voice to describe what happened to the girls, without identifying any perpetrators.[4]

On the second day of the story, Tuesday, 16 July, information about the rapes was almost entirely absent from all three local papers, despite continued extensive coverage of the crime. Nor was commentary included on the gendered nature of the crime. In the *Daily Nation* for that day a summary briefly mentions "reports of rape." Similarly, *The Standard* notes that "the invading boys assaulted and raped several girls before escaping into the bush." The *Kenya Times* only mentions rape via a secondary source (toward the end of the story), the chair of the Kenya Business and Professional Women's Club, Mrs. Beth Mugo, who condemns the boys for "sexually abusing" the girls. She also is quoted toward the end of the *Nation* story, but as expressing shock at the boys' brutal acts, with no mention of sexual violence.[5]

The emphasis in all three 16 July stories is on an ultimatum from Meru District Commissioner (DC) Peter Saisi that parents bring their sons and daughters to the school by 19 July—the boys for "screening" and the girls for assignments to new schools, as a decision to move the girls had been made by 15 July. All three papers continue to use quotes by President Moi and other government sources to frame the "tragedy" as the result of indiscipline. Underlying causes most frequently mentioned are incompetent administrators and teachers, though one source in the *Daily Nation* blames drugs and alcohol and another calls for an end to mixed-sex schools. Only *The Standard* uses eyewitness accounts obtained by going to Tigania Hospital and interviewing four victims recovering there. The four girls (who are named) talked about their injuries, the sequence of events, and the trauma of seeing their friends killed. There is no mention of rape in their accounts.[6]

The marginalization of rape and gender violence in the 15–16 July news stories extends to two editorials that first appeared on 16 July in *The Standard* and the *Daily Nation*. Although rape is mentioned in passing in these pieces, the overwhelming emphasis is on eliminating school discipline problems and on catching the leaders responsible, not on acknowledging or examining gender violence, as illustrated in the following from the *Daily Nation*. "A full investigation, followed by severe punishment of the psychotic hooligans who perpetrated Sunday's horror tragedy at the St. Kizito Secondary School is, we hope, merely the beginning of a thorough re-examination process of the discipline aspect in schools' curriculum and national ethos."[7]

The fact that rape crimes occurred could not be avoided for long by the Kenyan media, and was even in a *Daily Nation* headline by 17 July. However, the initial near-exclusion of the word rape in stories of this major crime does indicate the strength of the hegemonic perspective. Once rape got into the news about St. Kizito, it was explained primarily by government concerns about indiscipline (and related concerns) for weeks following the crime, though other explanations also surfaced. These explanations served as frames that reinforced patriarchy by taking up most of the media space and hence masking the reality of rape and the assailants' culpability.

Emphasizing Government-Source Explanations: Indiscipline, "Plotters," Mismanagement

As noted in the previous section, initial news about St. Kizito both ignored the gender violence that occurred and set the stage for the framing of the crime in much subsequent coverage. Media framing emphasized the government agenda, as established by President Moi. In Kenya, a long history of government control of media made the emphasis on government sources practically automatic in this major story, especially in the semi-official *Kenya Times*. Government influence on press coverage also reflects the sensitivity of the time period, which was prior to the December 1991 announcement of multiparty politics and the 1992 elections. Newspapers did print stories contrary to the government view, but usually did so cautiously and when the weight of public opinion was behind them. The Moi government had been concerned for some time about strikes in secondary schools and universities. So government sources framed the crime as "indiscipline" or a plot by foreign agitators. This agenda was transmitted in early international reports, which relied heavily on the local reports.

On 16 July President Moi, accompanied by many officials, personally toured the "death chamber," visited injured girls, and spoke to a large *baraza* [public meeting] at Tigania stadium near the school. He expressed outrage and concern for the victims and their families. His remarks, quoted in all three Nairobi papers on 17 July, again labeled the incident "indiscipline" and placed it in the context of twenty-one other recent strikes in the district. He announced that he would appoint a national committee to recommend ways of managing schools and instilling discipline and morality. He also used the occasion to castigate leaders who are poor role models for youth. He continued to talk about routing out the perpetrators, and directed local authorities to quickly find suitable schools for the surviving victims.[8]

Moi did not mention rape in his remarks, though rape is mentioned elsewhere in 17 July stories. The *Daily Nation*'s large front-page headline finally acknowledges rape: "71 Girls Raped in St. Kizito Tragedy." The story, by Imanene Imathiu, reports in the lead that doctors had confirmed seventy-one girls were raped. Only the headline and the lead mention rape, however, with a failure to state that St. Kizito boys committed the rapes. The remainder of this story deals with other issues: causes of death, conditions of the injured, expressions of condolences, and an announcement of a memorial mass. On page two the *Daily Nation* ran another story, headlined, "Leaders Condemn Girls' Killing." This story quotes seven high-ranking men—cabinet ministers, educators, church leaders—who blame the crime on indiscipline, "destructive foreign influences," the failure of mixed schools, poor dialogue between staff and students and financial mismanagement.[9]

The indiscipline theme gathered strength on 18 July when the *Daily Nation*'s page-one headline read: "Team Named to Probe Indiscipline in Schools." The *Kenya Times* also led with a story on the team. The eleven-member committee was to be headed by Mr. Lawrence Sagini, the chairman of the University of Nairobi Council and the Kenya Power and Lighting Co., and was to report its findings in three months. Members included church leaders, educators, and scholars. They also included two women, a nurse administrator, and a professor. The minister of education, Mr. Peter Oloo Aringo, gained a strong voice in stories on the team. He said that discipline requires better management and that the government would now require headmasters to reside in schools. He also said that the committee would examine school finances. Finally, he suggested that subversive factors could be involved in student unrest, for example, that "subversive elements could provide students with drugs and incite them to rebel."[10]

The idea of subversive elements undoubtedly came from the government's desire to attack critics of the ruling party. It was mentioned in the *Daily Nation* story, as noted above, and gained a front-page story of its own in the *Kenya Times:* "Aringo: Plotters Responsible for Children's Riots." *The Standard* gave the idea some space with the headline, "St. Kizito Boys Were Not Alone, Claims MP," which attributes the idea to the MP for Igembe, Mr. Joseph Malembe. The idea of outside agitators as responsible for the crime did not take hold as a major theme, however, and was not picked up by the international press;[11] nor did the international press use St. Kizito to criticize KANU or promote multiparty politics. When the outside agitators theme failed, government sources tried blaming politicians or church leaders (critics of government) for being poor role models, though this never became a major theme either.[12]

The dominant "cause" addressed in the local media for the first several weeks remained the government's concern with indiscipline and its presumed roots in poor management of schools and incompetence, misuse of finances, and poor dialogue. These latter themes also appear in international reports.[13] These issues do have relevance. But they typically were presented in ways that appeared to excuse the assailants' crimes, without an accompanying discussion of gender violence in society or the suffering of the victims.

Themes of incompetent administrators are prominent in feature articles which appeared the weekend following the crime in the three local papers. All three features quote the minister for education, Mr. Aringo. Additional sources in the *Daily Nation* feature include the director of education, Professor James Waithaka, Mr. Julius Mwangi of the Nairobi Primary School Heads Association, and Mr. S. K. Kibe, the secretary of the Kenya School Heads Association. Mr. Kibe, quoted at length, argues that the role of the headmaster is crucial, and therefore he usually is responsible for strikes. Mr. Kibe also points to poor communication between head teachers and students and the community, a failure of head teachers to live in the school, and disgruntled teachers who undermine headmasters by inciting students to strike. As time went on, incompetent head teachers also dominated local coverage of the research carried out by President Moi's team on indiscipline.[14]

The "inexperience" of the St. Kizito headmaster in particular was a topic of several stories, which indicate that parents and area residents had not been pleased with him. Not surprisingly, Mr. Laiboni, headmaster, and Mrs. Joyce Kithira,[15] the deputy headmistress, were suspended. Later, Mrs. Kithira was reinstated but demoted to the level of teacher and assigned to a different school. Mr. Laiboni was permanently sacked by the Ministry of Education. The Meru branch of the Kenya National Union of Teachers (KNUT) criticized the sacking, saying that Mr. Laiboni likely could have done little to prevent the crime and that he was a scapegoat for the ministry, which had "failed in its supervisory and inspectorate roles at St. Kizito."[16]

Poor dialogue often was emphasized by government sources concerned with indiscipline, with Mr. Mathew Adams Karauri, the assistant minister of education, a major spokesperson for this problem. This also was a frequent preoccupation of letter writers, including a "concerned parent," whose contribution was placed in a feature section of *The Standard.* Numerous stories, letters, and editorials (including most of those noted above) further specify financial mismanagement and high fees as catalysts of strikes. Many leaders quoted called for an examination of schools' financial records and fee structures. As with the poor headmaster/poor dialogue arguments, these often appear to excuse the assailants, and seldom consider gender violence in the society as a whole. One proponent of this explanation is Mr. S. K. Kibe, who notes that some school heads embezzle student fees, resulting in shortages of food and other supplies. Mr. Kibe assumes that students who lack sufficient food may understandably lack impulse control. "As we know, a hungry man is an angry man," according to Mr. Kibe.[17]

In sum, then, the extensive early news reports about St. Kizito are dominated by the political agenda of government sources, and do not include an analysis of gender oppression and violence in society. Leaders of Kenyan women's groups lacked the status of other leaders and were almost totally ignored as sources by reporters. St. Kizito therefore gave the government a convenient platform to oppose school strikes and "indiscipline," and to blame school heads and foreigners for the situation. In this way, even as the rape crimes became more evident in media reports, patriarchal ideology about rape was reinforced by media framing that deflected attention away from interpretations that would challenge patriarchy. "Indiscipline," however, was an insufficient diversion. It also lacked credibility among many who, while not willing to contest patriarchy, sought opportunities to challenge other aspects of hegemony. The key competing explanation, promoted by many, was the stress caused by the educational system in the country.

Emphasizing School-Critic Explanations: Stress and 8-4-4

The idea that academic stress caused the "tragedy" was first suggested, though minimally, by 16 July. The culprit in stress arguments is usually the 8-4-4 system of education, which, as previously described, had dropped one year from the pre-university curriculum without an accompanying drop in requirements. The first year in which the 8-4-4 change was implemented was 1978, and so secondary school students in 1991 were among the early cohorts to move all the way through the new system. Many complained that although a year was dropped from the curriculum, no subjects were dropped, and new subjects were added. Hence, many students and parents felt that the 8-4-4 system produced near-impossible academic expectations and great stress.

The first local mention of this possible cause is a *Standard* story, which quotes minister of health Mr. Mwai Kibaki, criticizing the 8-4-4 system. "Are students therefore 'cracking' mentally?" Kibaki asked. School frustration (hence stress) also is the main theme in a 16 July AFP story headlined "Kenya's Social Tensions Highlighted by Schoolgirl Killings," the second international story in my NEXIS sample to use primary sources. The author, David Chazan, interviewed Gitobu Imanyara, award-winning advocate for press freedom and multiparty democracy. Imanyara attributes the incident to "frustration at a broken-down school system." Imanyara also used the interview to highlight the anger felt by Meru, Kikuyu, and other groups excluded or distanced from power in the Moi government, suggesting that ethnic frustration played a role in causing the incident. Chazan additionally interviewed Bishop John Njue of Meru, who blamed the crime on school-related stress, and the Meru DC, Peter Saisi, who blamed drug-taking.[18]

In early stories the Minister of Education strongly rejected the view that 8-4-4 stress caused school riots.[19] As this theme became increasingly prominent over the two weeks following the crime, President Moi stepped in and castigated the media for contributing to future strikes by reporting it. Moi's statements appeared in all three papers, though the *Kenya Times* story is the most detailed. Moi warned of stern action if the nature of the reporting didn't change. In the *Kenya Times* story, the president directed his criticism specifically at the *Daily Nation* and the *Kenya Times*. According to Moi, "the local dailies have acted as paragons of virtue insinuating that something must be terribly wrong with the country's educational system while apparently suggesting that the government was doing nothing to arrest what they [the newspapers] see as a future national catastrophe resulting from countrywide strikes."[20]

Hence, it is clear that stories about 8-4-4 stress reflect resistance to the dominant view that indiscipline was to blame. However, dissatisfaction with 8-4-4 was so widespread that even two *Kenya Times* opinion columns dared to suggest that the system should be reviewed.[21] Given the extent of dissatisfaction with 8-4-4, the St. Kizito crime provided an opportunity for many to say so. However, as with the government agenda, this particular public sentiment often was reported in a way that appeared to explain away the crimes. While many stories included 8-4-4 stress as a factor in student strikes, some stories and letters focused exclusively on the 8-4-4 issue.

Especially notable is a story that appeared in the *Daily Nation* on 20 July, headlined, "Doctors Link Meru Tragedy to Stress." The lead paragraphs of the story quote the Kenya Medical Association (KMA) doctors' view that stress caused by 8-4-4 must be examined as one significant factor in the "tragedy." "The KMA said Kenya's educational system cannot escape scrutiny and whatever system is used, children must be allowed to be children with time to play: 'As doctors and parents, we have noted with grave concern the very heavy schedules given to children under the present system of education.'"[22] Many other groups, including educators and church leaders, were similarly quoted in subsequent stories in the three local papers. Numerous letter writers also made connections between the crime and 8-4-4. Although the 8-4-4 system is the major cause assumed in stress arguments, other arguments also were occasionally made, as in a *Sunday Nation* story, which suggests that the St. Kizito boys were especially stressed at the time of the incident due to a recent meningitis outbreak and their extremely overcrowded dormitories.[23]

Occasionally the 8-4-4/stress problem is linked with another problem to argue for an interaction effect, as in one *Kenya Times* story, which suggests that the 8-4-4 system increased risks associated with mixed-sex schools because it reduced the age and therefore maturity of the oldest girls. The story suggests that under the old system girls were more mature and did not so easily succumb to "cheap and simple romantic gestures."[24] Of course, this entire argument accepts the myths that rape is sex and that the victims deserve their fate, myths that will be discussed later in relation to the local stories.

In general, as a framing technique, 8-4-4 supports patriarchy in at least two ways. Like indiscipline, it provides an explanation that diminishes the assailants' culpability and diverts attention from possible feminist arguments. In some applications, it supports patriarchy quite directly by accepting rape myths. At the same time, it is noteworthy that these arguments contested the government efforts to ground explanations in "indiscipline" and to protect the basic educational system from criticism.

Reinforcing Ethnic Prejudices: "The boys never meant any harm . . ."

Another media frame that served to reinforce patriarchal hegemony by excusing the behaviors of the assailants draws on information about attitudes and behaviors in the Meru area, where the crime occurred. This information suggests that rape and gang rape are consistent with values indigenous to the Meru ethnic group.

Before continuing, it is important to emphasize that issues of ethnicity, culture, and sexual violence are complex and contain many contradictions. This is because, on the one hand, previously noted studies have demonstrated a greater propensity for rape and gang rape in societies that equate masculinity with dominance, tolerate or encourage violence as a means of solving problems, and discourage male involvement in child rearing.[25] Hence, media reports of such correlations may support the feminist goal of raising public consciousness about gender violence. On the other hand, a cultural perspective may mask the reality that rape and gang rape occur everywhere. It can also be used as an excuse for those guilty of violent crimes, and may support dangerous and misleading ethnic prejudices.

Helen Benedict demonstrates that rape crimes tend to evoke and exaggerate prejudices and myths related not only

to gender, but also to race and ethnicity.[26] Therefore, reporters attempting to blame indigenous values must do so
with extreme caution. If done well, via in-depth interviews
with appropriate local sources, this line of reporting may be
very important in placing a crime in its proper context—in
contrast to most of the reporting described thus far, which relies on urban sources who have their own agendas. However,
if not reported well, information about cultural norms may reinforce or create ethnic prejudices. This may have occurred
with regard to the Meru ethnic group. The St. Kizito crime
also likely evoked prejudices with regard to the continent of
Africa, as a result of the widespread use of material from a
Kenya Times story that described rape as commonplace in the
Meru area.[27]

In stories on St. Kizito, there were two types of ethnic-re-
lated explanations. The first, which was less significant, relates to the headmaster's ethnicity versus the ethnicity of the
community. The second relates to a sub-culture of violence,
which local sources and "experts" said characterized the Meru
area.

Headmaster's ethnicity. This possible contributing factor was
discussed only in the *Sunday Nation* and was not even mentioned in other papers. In a 21 July feature by education editor
Wamahiu Muya, the previously quoted Mr. S. K. Kibe, secretary of the Kenya Secondary School Heads Association, states
that if poor rapport exists between a headmaster and local
leaders, these leaders may incite students to strike to discredit
the headmaster.[28] He suggests this was likely at St. Kizito because the headmaster belonged to a different clan than that of
the local people. This difference was elaborated in a second 21
July feature, which points out that while the school was located in Tigania, Mr. Laibon, a Meru, belonged to the Igembe
clan of Kangeta location. Mr. Laibon's predecessor had been

from Tigania. According to the author, it is common knowledge that "the two clans are traditional rivals and clan affiliations count a lot in the district when it comes to where one should work." To back up this statement, the area district officer was quoted: "The local people were allegedly opposed to a foreigner managing the best of their schools. At the same time land border conflicts were going on between the Igembe and Tigania clans to which no solution seems to be in sight, according to the District Officer (DO) of the area. Some people in Tigania are opposed to Mr. Laibon simply because he is from Igembe. 'Believe it. It happens here,' said the DO. 'Clannism is a major political factor in Meru,' he added."[29]

Given ongoing government efforts to curb ethnic prejudice, it is interesting that the *Sunday Nation* reporters make an argument supporting appointments based on ethnicity. It is also worth noting that in Wamahiu Muya's 21 July feature, Mr. Julius Mwangi of the Nairobi Primary Schools Association offers a contradictory analysis. Mwangi suggests that the appointment of headmasters often is based more on politics and ethnicity than on competence, resulting in poorly administered schools.

The issue of the headmaster's ethnicity was raised only one more time, this time by Mr. Laiboni himself during a court appearance. In his testimony, Mr. Laiboni was quoted saying that the local community disliked him because he came from Igembe. He also said that the community was unhappy when he made the decision to enroll more than fifty students from outside the area.[30]

Subculture of violence. This theme appeared primarily in the *Kenya Times*, with scarcely a mention in the other two papers. Ultimately, however, it became a significant factor in the accused boys' defense, as well as in international stories.[31] The first mention is in a *Sunday Times* editorial opinion of 21 July, in which Mugambi Karanja discusses research by criminologist and Meru district probation officer Francis Macharia Apollos (who later testified for the defense at the trials), indicating that parts of Meru district have long been noted for high rates of murders, rapes, and other extreme violence, often arising from petty matters such as a debt of two shillings. He links his observations in part to the circumcision ritual, which he believes teaches boys that the highest value is toughness and that interpersonal violence including rape is justified to "uphold one's dignity."

> Mr. Apollos says he has found that the sources of all this disproportionate violence in these parts of Meru is the strong traditional values, customs and beliefs which at their core indoctrinate men "to be men"—meaning to be hard an [*sic*] unyielding and regard submission or compromise of any kind as extreme cowardice unworthy of anyone who would call himself a circumcised man . . . . Use of violence is therefore seen, he adds, as necessary for the sake of upholding one's dignity and standing with his peers. And, more chillingly, the users of the violence do not have any guilt feelings to deal with because whatever act they perpetuate is justifiable under their cultural norms.[32]

This editorial helped lay the groundwork for Alex Riithi's front-page story of 24 July, which was widely quoted internationally: "Another St. Kizito Shocker: Questions that Weren't Answered."[33] (See Appendix B.) Riithi quotes the school's headmaster, James Laibuni, deputy headmistress, Mrs. Joyce Kithira, several local residents, and Mr. Apollos, the above noted criminologist, to argue that rape was a common occurrence at the school and in the area, hence explaining why no one came to the aid of the girls. Many people heard the noises, but they were familiar noises. James Laibuni was the first source quoted:

> "In the past, the boys would scare the girls, out of their dormitories and in the process they would get hold of them and drag

them into the bush where they would 'do their thing' and the matter would end there, with the students going back to their respective dormitories."

"I believe none of the boys intended to kill. . . . This must have been a joke turned nasty. The boys just wanted to have a nice time with their girls and this has been the case whenever there were disturbances in the school in the past."[34]

Similarly a local resident stated that she had frequently woken up in the past to find that "there was nothing serious, but only the raping of the girls by the boys." According to Riithi, "This *laissez-faire* attitude towards sex was also exemplified by the explanation of the tragedy by the school's deputy head-mistress, Mrs. Joyce Kithira, who told President Moi when he visited the school: 'The boys never meant any harm against the girls. They just wanted to rape.'"[35] Riithi's evidence for a link between such statements and the indigenous culture includes the research of Mr. Apollos and local accounts: "For example, one old man had this to say regarding rape: 'In our days whenever I did anything like this, and it was reported to my parents, my mother used to get very happy for this is how she knew in me she had a man in the making . . . but nowadays you do it and you are rushed to court.'"[36]

Riithi concludes that the rapes and murders were caused by the cultural attitudes of the area. Otherwise, "there must have been a well-organized syndicate, probably under oath, to perpetuate the cruel and beastly act." This unlikely alternative explanation is (not surprisingly) consistent with the view of the minister of education, previously reported in the *Kenya Times*, though Riithi presents no evidence for it in his story.[37]

The cultural explanation and the deputy headmistress's quote—"The boys never meant any harm against the girls. They just wanted to rape"—had a significant impact on subsequent local reporting, on the trials, and on the international press. There were scarcely any published voices challenging or qualifying the popular view that rape is commonplace in Meru due to cultural learning. Yet the government's own descriptive analysis of Meru society, which states that values of self-control, respect and sexual temperance are inculcated at circumcision (discussed in chapter 2), contradicts the popular view and therefore suggests a need for critical analysis. In fact, I did not find one Kenyan or international story documenting and critically assessing the contradictory accounts.[38]

In addition, the validity of Riithi's account was never seriously challenged, yet its accuracy is suspect. Riithi's stories on St. Kizito are characterized by unsubstantiated statements and by some inaccuracies.[39] Also, the headmaster, James Laiboni, later vehemently (and in writing) denied that he ever said rape was commonplace at St. Kizito. He denied that rape occurred at the school prior to the crime, called the report malicious and accused Riithi of fabricating everything. Yet numerous local and international reports freely repeated Riithi's account.[40]

The sensationalism of the information in Riithi's story certainly increased its appeal and use, even though the information may have been inaccurate, was not accompanied by critical discussion, and could reinforce ethnic prejudices. In international reports, the information could support global prejudices about Africa.[41] At the same time, it is important to recognize that the quotes were valuable politically for women's organizations and feminist reporters seeking to educate audiences that rape is indeed a globally commonplace and greatly neglected crime of gender violence. This was certainly a major reason for the use of Riithi's material in some of the international, as well as local, stories.[42]

Even these feminist stories, however, may have evoked or

exacerbated racial or ethnic prejudices. Helen Benedict's analysis of the "wilding" concept in the reporting of the Central Park jogger rape suggests it evoked racial prejudices. Likewise, the *Washington Post* headline, "When Women Are Prey," may be viewed as implying that males (in Africa) are predatory animals. A *Chicago Tribune* story used a quote from a St. Kizito girl calling the assailants "a pack of hungry hyenas," a quote that did not appear in Kenyan newspapers.[43]

A less ambiguous international example is Sheryl McCarthy's *Newsday* opinion article headlined, "Cavemen Try Taking Women Back in Time: The Stone Age." In her column, McCarthy assumes the validity of reports that "rapes of schoolgirls by schoolboys were commonplace and should be expected," as well as the Western stereotype of African women as little more than "beasts of burden." Further, while McCarthy clearly intended to label all rapists "cavemen," she drew on existing prejudices about Africa as "uncivilized" or "stone age" to argue that rape everywhere is uncivilized.

> In this country, we assume that most African women hold a position slightly below that of farm animals, that their societal role is confined to being sexual objects, beasts of burden and bearers of children. But even knowing this, an attack of this kind boggles the mind. . . .
>
> One would hope at this point in history that relations between men and women would be more civilized than they were in pre-history.. . . The truth is that the caveman mentality still thrives. One sees it in the brutality of incidents like St. Kizito, St. John's, and the Palm Beach rape of which William Smith Kennedy [*sic*] stands accused. The boys involved didn't hit the girls over the head with clubs, but at St. Kizito, they literally dragged them into the bushes to ravish them.[44]

Clearly, in the case of St. Kizito, media frames involving ethnicity or race are complex and contradictory. Perhaps it was these unresolved contradictions that increased their appeal, particularly the appeal of the subculture of violence theory presented in Alex Riithi's *Kenya Times* story. John Fiske has argued that the popularity of texts depends in part on unresolved contradictions that audience members can "exploit" according to their social relations and identities.[45] Though Fiske refers primarily to television, it seems likely that the multifaceted impact of Alex Riithi's story illustrates this process. In this instance, whether accurate or not, the story was used at times to challenge patriarchy, as well as to reinforce patriarchy. It also supported certain ethnic and racial prejudices.

Reinforcing Patriarchal Rape Myths

As rape became more a part of the local news stories about St. Kizito, the unchallenged presence of rape myths became increasingly apparent, a presence that blatantly served to support patriarchal hegemony and to sympathize with the assailants. Hence, these myths may be viewed as a fourth framing technique. Consider, for instance, the following headline: "St. Kizito: 4 Girls Had Sex, Court Told," which accompanies a trial story reporting laboratory evidence that four of the girls who died had been raped. In another trial-related story, a defense witness (the previously noted Mr. Apollos), was unchallenged in his contention that some of the St. Kizito girls were lovers of some of the teachers. Therefore, "the offence [*sic*] was committed in the heat of passion that followed the provocation by the girls."[46]

As illustrated in the first example above, the myth that rape is motivated by a desire for sex surfaced frequently in stories and in letters to the editor. Related myths about the victims' roles (that they deserve rape because of their behavior or reputation) seem impossible to employ in this incident, given the large number of victims involved and the circumstances of the crime. Nonetheless, even these myths are evident in local stories, as in the second above example. Both types of myths are most evident in relation to certain issues that the crime evoked, especially the issue of mixed-sex schools and also issues of religion and morality, which arose in part because St. Kizito was a Roman Catholic school. Those concerned about mixed schools assume that teenagers (especially boys) cannot control their sexual urges. Hence, mixing teen boys and girls in schools invites disaster. Those concerned about religion and morality assume that premarital sex is a sin. Therefore, the St. Kizito incident indicates declining moral standards, pointing to a need for better religious training in schools and society. Proponents of both concerns assign blame for the crime not to the assailants but to the school system (in its failure to consider biological inevitabilities), to the church (in its failure to teach morality), and to the victims (in their presumed failure to resist immorality).

Mixed schools. From the outset of the local coverage, many sources blamed the crime—and other incidents of indiscipline—in part on the existence of mixed schools. Speaking two days after the crime, President Moi said that schools were mixed only for financial reasons, and that they pose special management problems. Stories quoting Moi and others to connect mixed schools with indiscipline frequently relied on myths that girls are responsible merely by being in the school (i.e., the victim is to blame) and that the presence of girls may result in uncontrolled lust in boys (i.e., rape is sex).[47]

In a lengthy *Sunday Nation* feature, headmaster James Laiboni said that managing a mixed school was taxing and that "the girls make special and expensive demands on the school."[48] Another *Sunday Nation* feature published on the same day suggests that there are "special disciplinary problems" in mixed schools which are grounded in the girls' attitudes and behaviors. "Sometimes the two sexes resent each other. Boys feel the girls look down upon them even at universities where many women date sugar daddies and outsiders rather than fellow students."[49] Likewise, a *Kenya Times* story suggests that girls are obsessed with catching boys, especially boys of wealthier family backgrounds. Hence they spend most of their time plotting strategies and worrying about fashion and make-up. The author, Mwicigi Njoroge, acknowledges that boys also are distracted by girls, but that girls are more affected "because of their temperament" and "because they are more susceptible to emotional disorders than the boys."[50] Other stories suggest additional stereotypic gender differences that render girls unsuitable for the same education as boys, as illustrated by the following *Daily Nation* letter, which called for an end to mixed schools: "Men and women are unsimilar in inclinations and dispositions. . . . Girls, for example, need to be trained not just as future career women but also as future mothers. The latter is of no relevance to boys and therefore the two should not be put on equal footing."[51]

A number of stories and letters reveal beliefs that mixed schools lead naturally to sexual behavior, as teenaged boys cannot control their sexual appetites. The Reverend Andrew Mungatia of the Meru Diocese stated in the *Daily Nation* that the late bishop who started St. Kizito never intended to admit girls but was pressured to do so by the government. This led to pregnancy and other problems.[52] In a *Kenya Times* editorial, Robert Otani suggests eliminating co-educational schools because sexual problems are inevitable and cannot be controlled no matter how the boys are punished, "like having a mule do as you bid." A *Kenya Times* letter writer, Willis Tsuma Musungu, argues that it is automatically dangerous to put adolescent boys and girls in school together, especially if the boys take drugs that cause "sexual mania." Some testimony given during the trials indicated a reliance on this assumption when it was alleged that "mischief" at night between the boys and girls had been common prior to the crime. A *Daily Nation* story in May 1992 profiled a school in western Kenya that had had the foresight (a year earlier) to eliminate sexual tensions and prevent a "tragedy" by moving the girls to new facilities, with dormitories, classrooms, and dining halls. One source in a *Daily Nation* story by Jane Some, Marianne King'ori, and James Wahome makes a very different argument, while still appearing to equate rape and sex. The authors quote Sister Catherine Salvini, who blames the St. Kizito incident on excessive *separation* of boys and girls, stating, "If Adam and Eve had not been forbidden the fruit, they probably would not have eaten it."[53]

It is noteworthy that the discussions of mixed schools focus primarily on sexual tensions between the genders with almost no attention to the fact that mixed schools opened up educational opportunities to thousands of girls. For example, the above-mentioned *Daily Nation* story about the "model" girls school in western Kenya notes only in passing that the new school lacks science facilities, so the girls must walk a kilometer away to use the laboratories at the boys' school. Exceptions include some discussion in the *Weekly Review*. Also, Jane Perlez makes this point in the second of her two stories for the *New York Times*.[54]

Morality and religion. In the local press the myth that rape is sex frequently interacted with the religious belief that premarital sex is immoral, resulting in stories that lament declining "moral" standards in youth. This was evident by the second day of news coverage in the headline accompanying a *Daily Nation* editorial, "Morals Were Never So Low in Schools," suggesting that the boys acted immorally because lust is immoral. Later stories often use religious metaphors and blame the crime on inadequate religious training. The fact that St. Kizito was a Catholic school encouraged these links. Several letter writers called for better religious instruction to encourage moral uprightness and hence eliminate such crimes.[55] Other sources making these links were church officials, who used St. Kizito to preach their views on sex and morality, and to call for more leaders with the same views. These views were summarized as follows in a *Sunday Nation* feature on the crime: "Declining moral standards in schools is another major problem. Churches have already complained that our schools lack a strong traditional disciplinary tradition because they are led by people who lack the correct spiritual and moral upbringing."[56]

Often, other complaints were mixed in with the idea of morality. For example, in a *Standard* story, Father Norbert Odero of the Catholic Archdiocese of Kisumu criticizes the 8-4-4 system for not leaving sufficient time for "pastoral guidance." He also blames government distribution of contraceptives among school girls, suggesting that "Giving the students contraceptives means that they should go around having sex with every Dick and Harry and Tom they fancy."[57] It is clear here that Father Odero places the blame on the girls by giving male names to the mythical sex partners. This leads to the cruelly inaccurate implication that the rape survivors committed sins.

In at least two other instances church leaders revealed similar ignorance of rape by comparing the dead girls to specific martyrs who died rather than commit a sin against chastity. Archbishop Zaccheus Okoth of Kisumu compared the dead victims to St. Kizito, who died rather than commit sodomy with the Kabaka Mwanga of Buganda.[58] In a letter to the *Kenya Times*, another priest and Italian missionary to Kenya, Pio Ciampa, S.J., blames the incident on inadequate instruction in the area of chastity: "St. Kizito's tragedy is a sign of the times and of the standard of sexual morality in our society!" He recalls Saint Maria Goretti, who at age 12 "preferred to be killed by a young man of 17 rather than to give in to his sexual violence." He also recalls an American missionary priest in Kenya who wrote a booklet on chastity for Kenyan youth, and he concludes: "I like to dream that the 19 victims of St. Kizito's had read his booklet and preferred to die rather than sin."[59]

It is important to point out that mixing religion with rape myths is particularly troublesome. The hegemonic strength of Christian values (in a largely Christian society like Kenya) certainly reinforces patriarchal hegemony as Christian leaders choose to interpret these values. For feminists, this poses added barriers, as it is hard to argue with religious leaders who represent a domain usually viewed as sacrosanct.[60] For victims, a lack of sensitivity by religious organizations may increase their pain and isolation by eliminating one resource that otherwise could be of great help.

Identifying Surviving Victims But Not Assailants

Identifying victims. The media identification of surviving victims (via names or photographs) is a simple framing device that can reinforce patriarchy by increasing victims' suffering and deterring other victims from reporting rape crimes. This issue has been controversial in the United States. In recent years, many newspapers have had policies against naming victims because of the stigma associated with rape. Nonetheless,

Illustration 3. Weekly Review cover, 19 July 1991. Photographer not named.
The cover is described as follows on page 2: "In dastardly acts of brutal
degradation, the boys of St. Kizito's Mixed Secondary School in Meru
District turn on the girls of the school in a frenzied attack that leaves 19
girls dead, 71 raped and over 80 injured."

victims often have been named, especially in more sensational cases, where one medium's decision to name results in competitive pressure on others to name.[61]

Benedict refutes several common arguments in favor of identifying victims. First, she argues that a "following the pack" line of reasoning—that if one medium names victims others may follow—is wrong because it presumes there is no principle at stake. Second, she disagrees with those who feel that naming victims will lend them credibility, asking why their credibility should be suspect and suggesting that the name is a "trophy for reporters." Third, she concedes that if the accused is named, some may feel it is fair to name the victim, too. She asks why the victim should *ever* be named but agrees that it may be fair to conceal the name of the accused until he has been formally charged. Fourth, Benedict takes issue with the argument that naming victims will destigmatize the crime. This takes the "rape is *not* sex" slogan too far by making it appear comparable to being pickpocketed, a crime completely free of sexual content.

> To deny the role of sexual humiliation in rape is to deny victims the horror of what they have been through. As long as people have any sense of privacy about sexual acts and the human body, rape will, therefore, carry a stigma—not necessarily a stigma that blames the victim for what happened to her, but a stigma that links her name irrevocably with an act of intimate humiliation. To name a rape victim is to guarantee that whenever somebody hears her name, that somebody will picture her in the act of being sexually tortured. To expose a rape victim to this without her consent is nothing short of punitive.[62]

During the year following the St. Kizito crime many female survivors (presumed or identified as rape victims) were named and portrayed in news photos in the three local newspapers and in the *Weekly Review*.[63] Precedents about identification were set during the first two days of the coverage. In the local reports a total of seven surviving victims were named in the first two days of coverage (six in stories and one in a photo), along with the nineteen who died. A number of survivors (one named) also appeared in photos—within the first two days in the *Daily Nation* and the *Kenya Times*, and in all three local papers by the third day.[64]

Altogether, in the *Daily Nation*, female survivors are named in twelve stories. Five photographs of surviving victims or their parents were published. *The Standard* names surviving victims in eight stories and used three photos identifying victims. The *Kenya Times* identifies surviving victims in six stories and in five photographs. The *Weekly Review* used a familiar photograph of victims recovering in Tigania Mission Hospital on its 19 July cover and used the same photo in three subsequent issues: in its 26 July issue, in its 9 August "Sexism in Kenya" issue, and yet again with a story in its 11 October issue. Surviving victims are named in the 19 July and 9 August issues. When quoted, the named survivors most commonly provide details about the night of the crime and about their injuries (aside from rape). When otherwise named, it is typically in the context of reporting on their injury status and location in the hospital at Tigania or Meru.

For obvious and justifiable reasons, the nineteen girls who died are named much more frequently than surviving victims, most often in the context of the crime itself or the memorial services. Some stories recall the personal merits and innocence of the slain girls, as in the *Weekly Review* of 19 July, which began with a description of Viola Karambu, one of the nineteen who died.[65] Occasionally, however, this naming is more sinister, as in Alex Rithii's widely quoted story of 24 July. In this story Riithi quotes a worker at the school who said the boys had a list of five girls who had "slighted them by

Illustration 4. The Standard front page, 30 July 1991. "Students deny 19 separate charges . . . St. Kizito tragedy: 29 boys in court," by Victor Nzomo. Photographer not named. Photograph shows smiling faces of three unnamed St. Kizito suspects. Other suspects are turned away from the camera.

befriending men from outside the school." According to this source, the outsiders, like the St. Kizito boys, were circumcised (implying they were now "men," therefore competitors for girls). Hence, "the boys had vowed to punish the girls even by death for . . . their behavior."[66] All five girls on the list died, and this information served no function other than to raise questions about the character of dead victims.

Double standard of identification. In contrast to all of the newspapers' eagerness to identify the survivors, they were extremely reluctant to identify the assailants. This decision was certainly due, in large part, to legal stipulations, which do not permit the publication of a minor suspect's name or school or other identification details, even after guilt has been determined. Kenyan law reads as follows: "No person shall publish the name or address of any person before a juvenile court, nor the name or address of any school which such person is or has been attending, nor any photograph of any such person, nor any matter likely to lead to the identification of such person, save with the permission of the court or in so far as is required by the provisions of this Act."[67] However, these stipulations were not adhered to by all publications nor were they met with complete compliance on the part of those who generally did adhere, as indicated in the exceptions I will note below. Suspected assailants *are* named illegally on occasion in the accounts. In addition, assailants are seldom named even when the law clearly would permit naming. For instance, some of the suspects (including those ultimately jailed) were over 18, yet they are seldom identified. In addition, there is no reason under the law why St. Kizito boys *not* formally accused (the vast majority) could not be identified, especially since surviving victims are identified. Yet these boys are almost never identified in the news accounts. Taken together, these observations suggest that a double standard of identification was not *necessitated* merely because the law existed and surviving victims were identified. Hence, this double standard, like the simple identification of victims, is vulnerable to feminist critique.

The double standard of identification was evident from the start. During the first three days of coverage in the local press, as documented above, many female survivors were named in stories or appeared in photos. Not one of the 306 St. Kizito boys was named in a story or appeared in a photo.

The *Daily Nation*, Kenya's most popular paper, did not identify any St. Kizito boys for many months after the crime occurred. One story of the arrest of twenty suspects following screening at the school names victims but not the suspects whom the story is supposedly about. Assailants were not named in the *Daily Nation* even after thirty were formally charged with manslaughter, and two of these also were charged with rape or attempted rape, nor after nine of thirty-nine original suspects were freed on bond.[68] The stories not only protect suspects' names, but describe them sympathetically, as follows:

> As each count was read out, the boys answered in turn "not guilty." They looked disheveled and their dark green and grey uniforms had turned brown with dirt.

> The sad-looking boy, dressed in a dirty white shirt, a blue water-proof jacket and grey trousers pleaded not guilty to each count. He was unrepresented.

> The boys, dressed in dirty uniforms, some in pullovers to ward off the cold, shivered in the dock and craned their necks as Mr. Ombonya delivered the ruling.[69]

Another example of the *Daily Nation's* sympathetic reporting is a 13 August story, headed "30 Kizito Boys 'In Thugs Den,'" which quotes the suspects' lawyers to state that "boys" were mingling with dangerous criminals at the Meru prison where they were being held. The lawyers had been arguing for weeks that the "boys" should be freed on bond. However, Meru authorities sharply refuted the *Daily Nation* sources, stating that the St. Kizito suspects were in a special juvenile section of the prison, were not mingling with adult criminals, and could be visited by their lawyers at any time. The *Daily Nation* dropped the charge, and it was never made by the other two papers.[70]

It is significant to note that the *Daily Nation*'s sympathetic stance toward the assailants continued through 1991 and the hearings and trials of 1992. Several stories in September discuss the move of boys not charged with a crime to new schools, including one mixed-sex school, and indicate great concern for their psychological and academic well-being. One story in October 1991 reports that the jailed "boys" were suffering from "a number of diseases, including scabies and 'infections in the private parts.'" In addition, assailants continued to remain unnamed in the *Daily Nation* even when the law would clearly permit identification. A front-page 19 February story by Imanene Imathiu reports jail sentences for four convicted assailants, all of whom had been determined by doctors to be 18 years old or older at the time of the crime, and hence not "boys" but "men."[71]

In the *Daily Nation* during the year after the crime, there were only three stories that named assailants, one technically legal, and two illegal. The former is a very short (3.5 column inch) KNA story of March 1992 stating that the four convicted criminals had been jailed.[72] Illegal identifications include two stories by Imanene Imathiu, each naming a different suspect. In a December trial story a Form III girl (named) describes being dragged outside but being saved by one of the suspects (also named). In an April story a former head boy at St. Kizito is named, and his testimony refuting that of two girls, also named, is extensively quoted.[73]

Unlike the *Daily Nation* stories, stories in the *Kenya Times,* *The Standard* and the *Weekly Review* about the suspects are relatively straightforward, with less editorial comment about their appearance or speculation about the conditions of their incarceration. However, these publications were similarly reticent to identify assailants, especially the *Kenya Times* and the *Weekly Review.* One of two photos of St. Kizito boys ever published appears in the 19 July *Weekly Review.* The photo is very small (bottom third of page), and the four boys ("trickling back to the school for screening") are unnamed and also unidentifiable due to photo size and poor print quality.[74] Two suspects—the school captain and his deputy, who both had been arrested—are illegally named in Alex Riithi's 24 July story.[75]

Otherwise, the *Kenya Times* did not name any St. Kizito boys or run photos of them, even after formal charges were brought. However, when nine suspects were released on bond because insufficient evidence against them could be gathered (though their bonded status meant they were considered a danger to society), both the *Kenya Times* and the *Weekly Review* did choose to name them. The *Kenya Times* named assailants two more times during the year following the crime —once in January 1992, when a suspect, illegally named, failed to appear in court, and again in February, when the four convicted assailants were jailed (they were named as well as eleven others who were tried).[76]

The Standard did not name any St. Kizito boys until formal charges were brought on 29 July, and then all twenty-nine suspects were named, though this is illegal. The front-page story on 30 July, which names the twenty-nine suspects, is accompanied by an unprecedented photo, showing about ten suspects (not named in cutline), three smiling and the rest with their backs to the camera. This page-one photo is the only photo of officially accused St. Kizito boys that appeared in any medium examined during the year included in this study. The photo and the story were both rather boldly illegal.[77]

How can the *Standard*'s decision to run this page-one photograph and name the juvenile suspects be explained? Perhaps the economic strength of the British corporate owner, Lonrho, alongside the *Standard*'s increasingly commercial orientation (compared to the *Daily Nation*) contributed to a willingness to assume greater risks in certain areas than the other papers were willing to embrace.[78] Whether gatekeeper(s) within the *Standard* had feminist motives in this decision cannot be known without interviewing those involved. However, it should be noted that not only was the 30 July page-one photo of the St. Kizito suspects unprecedented, it is one of only two occasions when photos of *any* accused or convicted rapists were published during the year of my study. In April 1992, Esther Kamweru, *Standard* managing editor, wrote an editorial feature denouncing an Easter Sunday sermon by Roman Catholic cardinal Maurice Otunga stating that women who dress scantily invite rape (Appendix C). The article was accompanied by four, clear frontal photographs of accused rapists (not St. Kizito assailants), all easily identifiable though not named. A photo of an unnamed victim with her head cropped off also was included.[79]

In addition to the 30 July *Standard* story and photo, when nine of the twenty-nine suspects (noted above) were released on bond, they also were named in *The Standard*'s story. Two additional *Standard* stories published during the year of this study name assailants. Both stories report on the trial of fifteen suspects, and named the four, convicted adult assailants sentenced to four years in jail each.[80]

In sum, the identification patterns point to support for patriarchal interests. Victims were identified, and they were identified more frequently than assailants. The most popular Kenyan paper by far, the *Daily Nation*, was most adverse to identifying assailants while identifying victims both in text and photographs. Assailants were virtually absent from photos in any of the papers, save two: the above-described *Standard* photo that included unnamed faces of a small handful of assailants charged with the crime; and a small *Weekly Review* photo with four unnamed, unidentifiable and not-yet-charged boys.

Although there were certainly legal reasons why minor offenders should not have been named (noted earlier), it is also clear that the legal standard was not always observed. Occasionally minor suspects were identified, with no known consequences for the newspapers. Even when the press *could* legally identify St. Kizito boys—as in the case of the boys not charged (the vast majority) and the convicted assailants over age 18—identifications were seldom made. Hence, as Patricia Stamp demonstrates, the law may not be as fixed as it seems, and uneven or discretionary applications of the law may work to favor certain interests.[81]

The impact on victims of identification alone or of the double standard of identification cannot be assessed in this research, but both point to a patriarchal insensitivity for the welfare of victims.

Suggesting Survivor-Assailant Equality via Labels

The labels used for suspects and victims in crimes, as well as names and descriptions of suspects and victims, may help reinforce patriarchal ideology, in this case by suggesting certain conclusions about their status and character and their relationships to one another. The terms "suspect" and "victim," for instance, themselves connote certain meanings. "Suspect" indicates a legal status, and may be subject to regulation, especially where children are involved. In the case of suspects under age 18, Kenyan law makes few stipulations about labeling, specifying only that the words "conviction" or "sentence" not be used to refer to children and young persons.[82] The term "victim" may be less accurate or desirable than a term suggesting empowerment, or movement beyond the experience of victimization—such as "survivor," a term I have tried to use with some frequency, as appropriate.

By far the most common labels for both assailants and surviving victims between 14 July and 31 August 1991 were "boys" or "girls," "students" and related labels such as "children," "teens," "schoolboys/girls." These tendencies are evident by scanning the stories' headlines (see appendix A). In the headlines, even the boys formally charged with manslaughter or rape are not once given labels such as "suspects," "the accused," or accused/suspected "assailants," "perpetrators," "rapists," "murderers," or "offenders." Twice, however, assailants are referred to as "rampaging boys," once as "riotous students," once as "dogs," once as "cavemen," and once as "riot boys." The girls are referred to as "victims" just twice and as "martyrs" once.[83]

I further quantified the use of labels in the three local newspapers and a subsample of the international reports by noting which labels for assailants and survivors were used in stories published during the first six weeks following the crime (table 3).[84] Again, it is clear that "boys," "girls," and "students" were the favorite labels. It also was fairly common for girls and boys to be labeled in relation to one another, for example, as "colleagues," "fellow students," or "classmates." This tone was set the first two days of media coverage, and continued thereafter. The relatively infrequent use of labels like "victim" or "survivor" for the St. Kizito girls and "suspect" or "accused," or suspected/accused (as appropriate) "perpetrator" or "assailant" for the St. Kizito boys masks the reality of the crime. The fact that both the assailants and survivors are mostly referred to in the same way—as "boys/girls," "school boys/girls," "male/female colleagues"—may be interpreted as suggesting equity, that really this was an "accident" involving equals, that is, groups equally victimized. This is certainly a perspective that the suspects' lawyers wished to convey, as is demonstrated in a quote by one of boys' lawyers, Mr. M. Karimi, who stated that the boys were merely "victims of circumstances." The fact that even the four assailants over age 18 who were found guilty and sent to jail were consistently referred to as "boys" is further evidence of the intent to convey equity. The terminology may additionally imply "boyish" antics not intended to cause harm.[85]

Table 3

Labels Used for Surviving Victims and Assailants,
14 July–31August 1991

	Daily Nation (N= 61 stories)		The Standard (N= 53 stories)		Kenya Times (N= 49 stories)		Int'l Reports (N=21 stories)	
assailants and survivors	M	F	M	F	M	F	M	F
boys or girls	37	43	27	29	30	41	20	20
children	7	5	1	3	2	6	1	1
teens/youth/juveniles	6	1	1	1	3	1	7	4
students/pupils	26	22	19	20	29	19	12	8
schoolboys or girls	5	3	5	3	1	13	3	8
colleagues, fellow students, classmates, schoolmates	3	9	5	4	14	18	4	1
brothers/sons or sisters/ daughters	3	10	—	4	3	12	—	—
assailants only								
suspects/accused	4	NA	5	NA	7	NA	1	NA
clients	3	NA	3	NA	1	NA	—	NA

Table 3 (cont'd.)

	Daily Nation (N= 61 stories)		The Standard (N= 53 stories)		Kenya Times (N= 49 stories)		Int'l Reports (N=21 stories)	
perpetrators/assailants/ offenders	2	NA	1	NA	5	NA	—	NA
marauding, rampaging or rioting: boys/invaders/men	12	NA	5	NA	5	NA	2	NA
culprits/criminals	6	NA	2	NA	7	NA	—	NA
those causing tragedy/ ringleaders	3	NA	2	NA	2	NA	1	NA
insane, mad or psychotic: boys/hooligans/rogues	1	NA	1	NA	7	NA	—	NA
unruly/ill-behaved boys	1	NA	2	NA	2	NA	1	NA
drug addicts/pushers	2	NA	3	NA	—	NA	1	NA
survivors only								
victims	NA	11	NA	6	NA	9	NA	1
dying/injured girls	NA	6	NA	1	NA	6	NA	1
frightened/terrified girls	NA	2	NA	—	NA	3	NA	—
helpless, defenseless or weak girls	NA	—	NA	2	NA	3	NA	—
innocent girls	NA	1	NA	4	NA	6	NA	1
martyrs	NA	1	NA	2	NA	2	NA	—
survivors	NA	3	NA	2	NA	2	NA	1

Note: The headings "M" and "F" refer to St. Kizito assailants (males) and sur-viving victims (females), respectively. The acronym "NA" is used for labels that do not apply because they refer to one group or the other exclusively. All stories about St. Kizito in the three local papers and "sister" Sunday papers were exam-ined between 14 July and 31 August 1991. International reports were those ap-pearing during the same time period and available in the database LEXIS/NEXIS as of August 1993, including the following: Agence France Presse (5), *New York Times* (3), Reuters (3), *Newsday* (2), *Los Angeles Times* (2), *Vancouver Sun* (1), *Ot-tawa Citizen* (1), *The Times* (London) (1), *Time* (1), *Christian Science Monitor* (1), *Chicago Tribune* (1). Besides labels in the table, labels used at least once each for the assailants in the Nairobi papers were: "shouting and screaming boys," "in-corrigible villains," "sad-looking boy" (*DN*); "beasts," "murderers," "wayward pupils," "bullish men," "strong men," "boy students-would-be-men," "brutal men," "striking students," "blood-thirsty boys," "mob of students," "innocent students" (*S*); and "beastly male colleagues," "young merchants of misery," "friends," "disgruntled boys," "unruly mob," "respondents," "'real men'" (*KT*). Other labels used at least once each for the survivors in Nairobi papers were: "heroines" (*DN*); "intended victims," "defaulting colleagues," "innocuous women," "Kenyans" (*S*); and "'their' girls" (*KT*). Labels used at least once for the assailants in international reports were "screaming boys" (AFP), "pack of hungry hyenas" (*Chicago Tribune*), and "cavemen," "high-spirited youth" (used by *Newsday*, 31 July 1991, for rapists in general, including the St. Kizito offenders). Labels used at least once for the survivors in international reports were "abused girls" (Reuters) and "sexual objects," "beasts of burden," and "bearers of children" (used by *Newsday*, 31 July 1991 for African females in general, including the St. Kizito girls).

In addition to conveying equity, labels were used to single out the "psychotic hooligans" responsible for the crime, beginning on 16 July, as argued in a *Daily Nation* editorial. The editorial calls for digging up the backgrounds of all boys in the school "to expose any budding psychos who may be masquerading as seekers of knowledge." Here, two common myths are used to support the government's emphasis on discipline: first, that it was really certain individuals, not all in the group, who raped, and second, that these few were insane. These myths, also consistent with a common media tendency to focus on individuals versus the group, are evident in the other two dailies as well. A *Standard* editorial the same day assigns guilt to "drug pushers" and "ringleaders." The school's headmaster, James Laiboni, is quoted saying that thirty-five of the boys were suspected drug addicts and the likely guilty ones. Also, an early *Kenya Times* story quotes President Moi saying that the majority of the country's youth are disciplined, save for a few "black sheep."[86]

Table 3 summarizes the use in the local press of labels that focus attention on particular assailants ("ringleaders," "drug addicts," "psychos," "rogues," "beasts"), who were likely insane or drug-addicted, and were *really* to blame for the crime[87]—in contrast to the group as a whole, which was best described as "unruly," "ill-behaved," "wayward" or "striking." Furthermore, the use of terms associated with battle like "rampaging," "marauding" or "invading" boys, though perhaps accurate, may reflect or evoke patriarchal beliefs about "normal" male behavior. Hence they may reinforce an empathic response from males who assume "boys will be boys," though in this instance things got out of hand.

Labels for the surviving victims other than "girls" or "students" or "classmates" were less frequent than for the assailants in the local reports. The survivors were far more often referred to as "sisters" or "daughters" than the assailants were as "sons" or "brothers," which may partially reflect a societal tendency to define females primarily in relation to males— that is, as sisters, daughters or wives.[88] Other labels used, though infrequently, were "dying" or "injured" girls, "helpless" and "defenseless" girls, "innocent" girls, "martyrs" and "survivors." (As noted earlier, the label "martyr" supports rape myths when used to connote sexual purity on the part of the victims.)

Labels chosen for participants in gendered conflict (and other linguistic choices) are not insignificant, in that they may support patriarchal hegemony evident in other forms, including sources quoted, information ("facts") emphasized, and myths evoked. In this case study, the adjectives and synonyms selected for assailants and surviving victims tend to deny or trivialize the horror of the crime, reinforcing the already present strong media bias toward assailants. This was done in two interrelated ways: by using language that equalizes the status of assailants and survivors (both local and international press), and by drawing on the myth that in gang rape only a few psychotic leaders are to blame (local press).

4

Feminist Framing

Showing Concern for Survivors

Given that the framing techniques discussed thus far serve primarily to reinforce patriarchy and protect assailants, to what extent do press reports show concern for surviving victims? The main way in which local reporters and their sources purported to show concern for the survivors was in their immediate assumption that the girls would best overcome their trauma by being moved quickly to new schools. This issue was not discussed in the international press. It has already been noted that a decision to move the girls to nine new schools was made within a day of the crime. All nine schools were girls-only schools. According to the *Daily Nation*, "The decision to transfer the girls was reached after a high-level two-hour closed-door meeting at the school. It was agreed that the girls would be unable to continue their studies at St. Kizito because of the grim psychological aftermath of the tragedy." The *Daily Nation* story names the deputy eastern provincial commissioner, Mr. Daniel Omangi, as the chair of this committee meeting, which reached this decision after interviewing "more than 20 teachers, including the headmaster and his deputy." Within less than two weeks of the incident, the girls had been assigned to nine new girls schools, all within Meru District.[1]

In reporting this decision official sources almost always express concern for the safety of the survivors and their psychological trauma. Also, stories (such as those noted above) indicate that parents were overwhelmingly in favor of the move. No story or editorial provides a depth discussion on possible costs or benefits of moving and separating the girls. However, some stories do note alternative viewpoints. In particular, a *Standard* story of 18 July reports the reactions of five named victims. Two victims are quoted opposing the move:

> "Transferring us will not serve any purpose. It is better if the boys are transferred instead. They are the ones to be punished and not us."

> "Let the boys go. Let us come back to the school. We are innocent."[2]

In the same story other girls express concern that they would never be accepted in their new schools and would always be thought of as the "rape victims." (Some letter writers also argued that the girls should not be moved, and that they would suffer because of the stigma of rape.[3]) Apparently in partial response to the *Standard* story, President Moi ordered a reconsideration of the hastily-made decision to move the girls.[4] However, there is never any indication that the transfers were in doubt, and all the sources quoted in transfer-related stories (mostly official sources and some parents) state unequivocally that the survivors should be moved to girls-only schools for their psychological well-being.

The psychological well-being of the boys also was the main

concern in a decision to move all of the boys out of St. Kizito, and to schools *outside* of Meru District. Within two months of the crime, 218 of the boys not charged were distributed in up to twenty schools in nine districts. Not all of these schools were boys-only schools, and Kangaru High School, a mixed school, received forty-three of the boys. There were no reports of reactions by girls at Kangaru School. The double standard at work in this decision is obvious. It was assumed crucial that the St. Kizito victims, but not the assailants, be moved to single-sex schools for their safety and psychological well-being. The welfare of girls in the mixed-sex school receiving St. Kizito boys was not addressed in news stories.[5]

In addition, given the purported interest in the well-being of the surviving victims, it is noteworthy that no stories in the Kenyan press indicate what type of counseling, if any, survivors received until a year later, when the *Sunday Nation* reported group and individual counseling by a new anti-rape organization, Mothers in Action. Further, the media showed little interest in the victims' academic well-being, and stories published a year later report their academic performance had fallen greatly, whereas the boys did quite well.[6]

From this brief account it is clear that media efforts to show concrete concern for victims were contradictory and insufficient. The media emphasis on moving the girls for their psychological well-being no doubt was well intended, but it is balanced by a near equal emphasis on moving the boys. Also there is almost no coverage of plans or actions (or a lack thereof) to assist the girls once moved. Reports of moving the girls also were likely sabotaged by media frames already discussed, particularly those involving rape myths and suggesting that girls should not have mixed with boys in the first place.

Feminist Resistance

Effective means of challenging patriarchal ideology include exposing the larger context of gender violence and oppression (consistent with socialist feminism) and/or by documenting and confronting specific public expressions of patriarchy, such as the dearth of women in high-level public positions or the safety of girls in schools (consistent with liberal feminism). To what extent were these overlapping themes present in the Kenyan media after the St. Kizito crime?

Examinations of St. Kizito grounded in feminist critiques of patriarchy did not emerge quickly in the Kenyan newspapers, and almost never gained front-page prominence. By the time feminist themes did emerge, their proponents had the additional task of countering all of the other explanations and myths that had been taking up so much space in the media. Nonetheless, St. Kizito did inspire considerable activism challenging women's oppression in general and violence in particular. This new activism had a significant impact on media and other arenas for public discussion.

The Standard was the first of the local print media to suggest that St. Kizito reflected a larger gender issue in society. This was done in a brief opinion piece by Oketch Kendo on 18 July, at the bottom of page 21, headed "An Example of Violence against Women." Kendo argues that St. Kizito cannot be analyzed as one more incident of student unrest. "How come those who died are all girls?" he asks. He tentatively suggests —"farfetched as it may sound"—that the event "is part of a sexist sickness symptomatic of a chauvinistic culture." This sickness is endemic to all "paternalistic societies," as illustrated by the 1989 murder of fourteen young women in Montreal. He notes that tougher gun laws were enacted in Canada, and he called for drastic action "to protect helpless women against brutal men."[7]

A day later, the 19 July *Weekly Review* contained a nine-page account of the incident and a strong editorial statement by the editor-in-chief, Hilary Ng'weno. According to Ng'weno: "But there is more to the St. Kizito incident than a mere breakdown in discipline in our schools. More graphically than any other event in recent years, this tragedy has underscored the abominable male chauvinism that dominates Kenyan social life. Despite what our laws say . . . the lot of our women and girls is lamentable. We treat them as second-class beings, good only for sexual gratification or burdensome chores. We bring up our boys to have little or no respect for girls."[8]

In the *Sunday Nation*, this argument was first tentatively made on 21 July, in a brief editorial by Mkanju, headlined, "Ministry Should Act Promptly over Children." The author recounts several reports of gender violence among Kenyan schoolchildren, including incidents of molestation: "Tom Sitima and his Provincial Education Officers (PEOs) know that boys molest girls in the schools . . . . Nobody has lifted a finger because there was no St. Kizito." He concludes, "But maybe we should be asking ourselves what is in schools that leads to Kizito? Are similar interpersonal relationships to be found in our homes?"[9]

Most subsequent such stories, including the first *Kenya Times* story to raise explicitly these questions (noted below), were instigated by women's organizational work that was granted increasing media space in August.[10] On 22 July, *The Standard* reported on a statement by the Association of Sisterhoods of Kenya (AOSK), which called for a change in societal attitudes toward women. The same day, the *Daily Nation* published a story headlined "Women Want More Posts." The story reports a statement by the KMYWO (KANU Maendeleo ya Wanawake Organization), a government-affiliated organization dedicated to the advancement of women, appealing to

President Moi to increase women representatives on district land boards and development committees, and uses the occasion to frame St. Kizito as a crime of gender violence. A few days later a *Daily Nation* story headlined "Women to Discuss Child Abuse" announced that all women's organizations had been invited to Maendeleo House to discuss child abuse and harassment issues highlighted by St. Kizito.[11]

The first *Kenya Times* story (apart from Riithi's reports of ethnic norms) to frame St. Kizito as societal violence against women was published on 1 August, also in relation to women's organizational work in the aftermath of the crime. The page-one story, headlined "Family Violence: Women's Bodies Take up the Cudgel," was written by Cecilia Kamau (the first woman to single-author a St. Kizito-related story). It announced a joint statement by the KMYWO and the Kenya Business and Professional Women's Organization (KBPWO); this statement also was the subject of stories in the *Daily Nation* and *The Standard*. However, the *Kenya Times* story was the most detailed in describing both the statement and the status of the injured girls and accused boys. Two days later, another *Kenya Times* story with color pictures also summarized the joint statement, though much more briefly.[12]

Given its significance, the joint statement is worth summarizing. The statement condemns the behavior of the students and administrators of St. Kizito school, defines the extreme seriousness of rape relative to other crimes, states that St. Kizito mirrors the kind of abuse and violence that Kenyan women and girls experience daily, refutes the assumption that violence against women is indigenous to any culture in Kenya (or anywhere), notes additional violence against women sparked by the crime, calls on voters to elect gender-sensitive leaders, calls upon women's organizations to sensitize society about the status of women, calls on the government to set up family courts to deal with violence against women and girls, and calls on all Kenyan adults to examine their own attitudes and behaviors.[13]

In August several other stories appeared in the three papers, all instigated by women, by women's organizations, or both. A memorial service for the dead victims at Consolata Catholic Church in Westlands, Nairobi, was organized by the KMYWO and the KBPWO and resulted in stories both announcing and reporting on the service. These latter stories report the remarks of participants, especially KMYWO chair Mrs. Wilkista Onsando and KBPWO chair Mrs. Beth Mugo, all of which frame the crime as gender oppression in society. In particular, Onsando read a statement by Kenya Women Organizing Committee of the Women Individuals, Groups and Organizations against Abuse and Violence, which was distributed to those present, calling for an end to violence against women and children. Portions of this statement were quoted in the various stories. The *Kenya Times* story by Cecilia Kamau, "Befitting Memorial for St. Kizito Girls," reports the event in the greatest detail.[14]

Three other newspaper stories in August, all by women, deserve special mention, as they demonstrate women's efforts to gain voice in the media. In the *Sunday Nation*, a 4 August opinion piece by Rasna Warah compares the St. Kizito crime to highly publicized crimes elsewhere, for example, the 1983 New Bedford, Massachusetts, barroom gang rape and the 1989 Montreal murder of fourteen female students: "All three are illustrations of deep-seated contempt of women, exacerbated by unbelievable apathy on the part of society." Warah points out that rape is not about sex, but about violence and humiliation: "I therefore do not subscribe to the much touted theory that rape is a result of 'indiscipline' because even the most disciplined armies in the world have committed this unforgivable crime. Rape is also used by insecure men to 'teach women a lesson' or to 'put them in their place.' And that is exactly what the boys at Kizito did."[15]

Later, a *Daily Nation* feature of 14 August by Martha Mbugguss reported in detail on a 29 July women's meeting on gender violence at Maendeleo House. The story quotes several experts to describe the reality of rape, including its grave impact on women and some resources for victims. The *Standard* also published a long feature, headlined "Kenyan Women Are Angry," on women's oppression in Kenya, including the prevalence and effects of rape and failures of the legal system. It is also important to credit the *Weekly Review* for its 9 August 1991 issue, titled "Sexism in Kenya: A Woman's Lot Is Not a Happy One," with seventeen pages devoted to detailed discussions of sexism in general, legal discrimination, rape and male dominance, women and education, and the feminization of poverty.[16]

Women's organizational activity against rape intensified in September and October 1991 with the formation of two new anti-rape organizations. The more prominent, called the Kenya National Anti-Rape Organization (KENARO), was announced on 12 October 1991 and registered on 17 January 1992. Its secretary general, Ms. Fatuma Abeya Anyanzwa, quickly became a national leader and spokesperson against gender violence, and she was subsequently quoted in numerous stories. Also, Mothers in Action formed quickly after the crime and generated media attention for its activism. At the same time, many already existing women's organizations shifted their focus increasingly to gender violence, with accompanying media coverage. Some even created new affiliated institutions, as did the Kenya chapter of the International Federation of Women Lawyers, which opened a free Women's Legal Aid Clinic to assist victims of gender violence.[17]

It became increasingly difficult for prominent leaders to promote rape or rape myths without strong objections by women and media coverage of these objections. For instance, in September 1991 the Nakuru branch KANU chairman was denounced by Mothers in Action for threatening at a public rally to "take and rape your wives you Kikuyus, like we did during the emergency if you follow multi-party advocates." Women's reactions were even stronger following Cardinal Otunga's previously noted Easter Sunday statement that scanty dressing invites rape.[18]

In sum, during the first few weeks after the St. Kizito crime, a perspective grounded in women's oppression in society did gain space in the Kenyan newspapers, primarily as a result of women's organizational work. Women's continuing efforts, including the work of two new anti-rape organizations, were responsible for increased space for feminist perspectives during the remainder of the year following the crime, especially in *The Standard*, the *Kenya Times*, and the *Weekly Review*. The stories did not (with the exception of one *Kenya Times* story and the 9 August *Weekly Review*) get on the front page. The fact that feminist perspectives gained some space is significant; and I have appendicized several stories to highlight their significance (Appendix C). However, interpreted in terms of hegemony theory, it is an example of accommodating feminist interests to some extent while continuing to report the crime in a manner favoring the dominant ideology. As Ms. Anyanzwa's voice became stronger, the predictable backlash occurred. She was jailed for her activism in September 1993, with considerable attention by the press.[19]

In the international press, the vast majority of the early reports focused on facts of the incident—that is, deaths, injuries, and arrests—presented in relation to the ongoing educational crisis in Kenya, with almost no reference to the gendered context of the crime or feminist activism. Feminist themes began to appear in late July and early August, drawing in part on the St. Kizito deputy headmistress's quote—"The boys never meant any harm . . ." from Alex Riithi's *Kenya Times* story.[20]

Jane Perlez's two *New York Times* stories were exceptional in providing important contextual details about the status of Kenyan women, information otherwise not present in the mainstream press for Western audiences. However, without accompanying information about Kenyan women's strengths, including their activism following the crime, even Perlez's otherwise commendable stories may have reinforced negative Western stereotypes of African women as victims. (Interestingly, this gap was rectified by *Women's International Network News*, which combined text from Jane Perlez' two *New York Times* stories with text from Cecilia Kamau's front page 1 August *Kenya Times* story on Kenyan women's activism.[21])

While Jane Perlez's stories provide some context, in stories lacking *any* contextual information the stereotyping becomes blatant and undermines the feminist intent when published in the Western press. Sheryl McCarthy's previously noted "Cavemen" editorial drew implicitly on Hilary Ng'weno's *Weekly Review* column, which calls for an analysis of women's oppression in Kenya. But, whereas Ng'weno's words were read by a predominantly Kenyan audience and prefaced an extensive report in the *Weekly Review,* McCarthy's characterization of African women as "beasts of burden and bearers of children" stood alone, hence reinforcing a Western stereotype. In contrast, it is appropriate to highlight one column, which uses primary sources, and is unusual in its efforts to emphasize Kenyan women's activism and explicitly reject Western stereotypes. The column, by Michele Landsberg, appeared in the *Toronto Star* three months after the crime: "Ripped out of all context, the story of St. Kizito boarding school was enough to revive hateful stereotypes of the Dark Continent. The story troubled me all summer. I was sure there was more to learn. What, for example, did the women of Kenya have to say? Surely they didn't accept this brutality in passive silence? But, as with so many international stories, this one sizzled like sudden lightning across the front page and then vanished into oblivion."[22] (See also Appendix C.)

After July and August of 1991, stories about St. Kizito indeed appeared only rarely in the international press. In the few stories that did appear, feminist themes were increasingly apparent, as in the above-quoted story. However, it is important to emphasize that these stories were few and far between compared to stories on other issues that emerged from the developing world, reports which in turn had to compete for space with "first world" news. The increasing prominence of feminist perspectives was due to the fact that the only reporters still interested in the crime after the first several weeks were those committed to educating audiences about gender oppression in society. Two noteworthy stories, not yet mentioned in this context, that discuss gender oppression drawing in part on the St. Kizito headmistress's quotes (from Alex Riithi's stories) and which also include discussions of women's organizational work in Kenya and globally, were both published in the *Washington Post*: one by Lori Heise in 1991 and one by Susan Okie in 1993. Some Inter Press Service stories also emphasized Kenyan women's activism in the aftermath of St. Kizito.[23]

In general, the feminist framing of the St. Kizito crime both challenged patriarchal frames (e.g., that "indiscipline" was to blame) and the common media tendency to focus on events rather than context[24] by exposing and confronting gender violence and oppression in society as a whole. The feminist resistance—both organizational efforts and media reports—

indicates consistency with critical perspectives in recognizing that St. Kizito is symptomatic of a complex pattern of gender oppression, no single aspect or expression of which can be addressed in isolation. Feminists (including some men) were able to get their agenda in the news primarily via editorials and letters. They also started organizations and created events and spokespeople that would generate news coverage. The amount of this coverage, however, was very small compared to that supporting patriarchal perspectives, and rarely given prominence. Hence, as others have argued, it is consistent with patterns and behaviors of expansive hegemony, which secures consent by incorporating small amounts of feminism while placing an overwhelming emphasis on reports favoring the dominant ideology.

5

Conclusions

Gender violence is a global reality that kills and injures millions of women and girls everywhere. Those not directly attacked remain affected by an ever-present fear of violence. The St. Kizito crime shows that girls struggling for an education are not safe even in school. This certainly is an issue of basic human rights, but it goes beyond human rights. Three-and-a-half decades of economic development have demonstrated the need for shared participation and decision-making power between men and women. Women's literacy and education are obvious prerequisites for women's participation and empowerment. Therefore, this study assumes that as long as the reality and fear of gender violence thwart the life, health and self-actualization of half of the human population, society as a whole is profoundly impeded.

This research further assumes that women globally need to seek common ground, while recognizing, respecting, and seeking to understand complex differences in experiences of gender oppression. This can be accomplished in many ways, including extending feminist scholarship beyond the boundaries of Western societies and examining similar questions in different cultural contexts.

Drawing on Althusser, Gramsci and others, I have argued that media and other ideological institutions constitute crucial sites where hegemonic perspectives are constantly reinforced and challenged. In the case of gender violence, media may support patriarchal hegemony via a wide variety of mutually-reinforcing framing techniques, which intersect with and are supported by news traditions and values. Media also may combat gender violence by responsible reporting (e.g., avoiding rape myths) and by reporting perspectives that call for accountability and change. Urban print media's power often is underestimated in developing countries, where the vast majority of the people live in rural areas and illiteracy is widespread. Yet, these media influence the educated, urban minority (including political leaders), who wield disproportionate power to effect change. They also serve as information sources for broadcast media and the international press. This research therefore extends prior scholarship on how media cover gender violence to developing countries by examining how patriarchal hegemonic process was revealed in press coverage of the St. Kizito crime.

This study identified seven framing techniques that served to support patriarchy in the print media's coverage of St. Kizito. These frames evolved over time as contradictions arose that needed to be accommodated. For instance, the media's initial instinct to ignore or minimize the rapes could not be continued as the extent of the rape crimes became widely known. The replacement strategies were to acknowledge and condemn gender violence, but to ground it in varied explanations (i.e., frames) that deflected attention away from the assailants' culpability and the larger context of gender violence and oppression in society.

These latter frames also changed and evolved over time. They included explanations of indiscipline due to mismanagement (the government's agenda) and of academic stress due to the educational system in the country (an agenda widespread among citizens, but contrary to the government's view). Media framing also included rape myths as they had evolved in Kenyan society. For instance, the common myth that rape is motivated by lust is reflected in stories blaming the crime on mixed-sex schools (historically controversial in Kenya) or on inadequate religious training (a subject of concern given widespread, conservative religious views). The myth that rape is culturally indigenous to certain groups is reflected in uncritical local reports about the Meru ethnic group and international reports that indicated racial prejudices. Other related frames were a double standard of identification and the use of language that equalized the status of assailants and surviving victims.

Despite the strength of the above frames and their support for patriarchal views of rape, there was evidence of alternative views. Some stories did express concrete concerns about the welfare of the St. Kizito survivors, especially their swift and smooth placement in new schools. These stories do not go very far, however, in considering various alternatives or the needs of the survivors following placement. More significant challenges to patriarchy are those stories revealing and critiquing pervasive gender violence and societal complacence regarding violence. These stories became more frequent over time, though they were rarely given prominence.

Initially, the few journalists raising feminist issues were male, most notably Hilary Ng'weno, editor of the *Weekly Review*, as there were no women reporters covering St. Kizito. These early feminist views were expressed primarily in editorials, as the reporters covering the crime did not seek leaders of women's organizations or rape experts as sources. The appearance of these editorials written by men is consistent with Gaye Tuchman's finding that marginalized groups or movements often must initially recruit established personnel within the mainstream to support their cause.[1]

As time went on, a few women writers and reporters, like Cecilia Kamau and Rasna Warah, went to great effort to educate the public on the reality of rape and on the perspectives of Kenyan women's organizations. Media attention was generated both by new organizations and by new initiatives of existing organizations. These stories did help fill a gap in the St. Kizito narrative. They also likely helped educate readers, which is always the first step for change. Likewise, some international reports have undoubtedly been important in raising global consciousness of gender violence in society, though some reports may have reinforced Western stereotypes of African women as passive victims, alongside stereotypes of African men as beasts. Michele Landsberg's *Toronto Star* column was exceptional in providing context without reinforcing stereotypes.[2]

In keeping with the work of expansive hegemony, expressions of feminist resistance were indeed overwhelmed by patriarchal perspectives during the year following the St. Kizito crime. At the same time, the efforts of individual journalists plus the establishment of new Kenyan women's organizations and their visibility (though still limited) in media indicated the increased *availability* of alternative meanings for those who wanted them.

In addition, the contradictions contained within patriarchal framing always provide openings for alternative interpretations. There are many examples in this research. For instance, accounts of rape as indigenous to the Meru ethnic group were used in Kenyan media both to excuse assailants and to make feminist arguments. Interviews with readers would undoubtedly yield a much more complex picture. John Fiske, among others, has argued that aside from the hegemonic work done by media texts, "there is still excess meaning that escapes the control of the dominant and is thus available for the culturally subordinate to use for their own cultural-political interests."[3] This excess meaning, that is, polysemy, can be used to nurture resistance movements and, in time, to influence the evolution of hegemony.

Although different cultural and historical contexts will certainly yield different framing patterns to support or challenge patriarchy, print media's coverage of the St. Kizito crime bears many similarities to observations of media's coverage of rape crimes in the United States. The three Kenyan dailies assigned the story to male reporters proximate to the crime, went to traditional and obvious official sources, indicated a focus on present events versus context and on individuals versus the group. They also were certainly influenced by economic considerations, which permit the coverage of rape events only when sensational in nature or when famous or upper-class people are involved. These behaviors, alongside the above-described framing techniques, resulted in stories that overemphasized patriarchal agendas and gravely neglected crucial contextual information: information on women's status in Kenya and globally. In addition, there was a loss of media interest after the initial shock wore off, so that the trials of the accused assailants and other events after the first few weeks received very little press attention.

As Benedict points out, media coverage that favors patriarchy serves not only to perpetuate it, but to cause possible further harm to survivors of gender violence and future survivors. Her recommendations for media certainly apply here, including: expanding the context of stories by seeking rape experts as sources, reporting feminist perspectives, avoiding rape myths, and not identifying victims—hence, avoiding a double standard of identification of assailants and victims. In addition, newspapers everywhere need to make more effort to diversify newsrooms and create policies on covering gender violence, policies that are presently very rare in developing countries.[4]

Finally, it is significant to note that while this study identifies and interprets news reports about the St. Kizito crime, important components of the process remain unexamined. I am hopeful Kenyan scholars will extend this research via interviews with reporters and editors, with key sources, with audience members, and, as appropriate, with those who experienced the crime first hand. Longitudinal studies of Kenyan media's coverage of gender violence up to the present also would be useful in indicating whether and how hegemonic process has adapted to new and bolder feminist challenges. It is additionally important for feminist scholars globally to monitor and critically examine their local media, and demand increased concern, attention and accountability from these institutions.

★ ★ No. 9618, Nairobi, Wednesday, July 17, 1991 Price KSh6/00

Death dormitory moves Moi to tears

By IRUNGU NDIRANGU

A sense of horror and poignancy overcame President Moi yesterday, moving him to tears as he surveyed the dormitory in which 19 girls of a Meru high school died during an attack by rampaging boys last Saturday.

In all his life, he had never witnessed "such an ugly incident where male students attacked their own sisters resulting in such loss of life."

President Moi told a huge crowd at a meeting convened next to the school.

After an extensive tour of the St. Kizito Mixed Secondary School in the morning, he said he was moved to tears when he saw what the girls went through in their dormitories on Saturday night.

It was a ghastly and beastly action, he said, and ordered security men to find out the reasons leading to the incident.

He particularly wanted to know why three watchmen armed with bows and arrows did not threaten to use force on the boys or even fire a single arrow to scare them away.

Similarly, he wanted to know why the watchmen ran away abandoning the girls.

The President said he had gone to Meru to offer his personal condolences and those of Kenyans to the families of the 19 girls.

The 19 girls have been identified as: Sarah Kamuri (Form 4), Elizabeth Nkatha (Form 3), Jane Kithure (Form 4), Margaret Mugambi (Form 3), Martha Mutuuma (Form 4), Rose Lucheon (Form 4), Nancy Gacheri (Form 4), Brenda Kiraga (Form 1), Lucia Karembu (Form 4), Edith Torome (Form 3), Judith Kabiriithi,

Dorcas Mwatuchu (Form 1), Tabitha Mwari (Form 1), Faith Gatchipioa (Form 1), Flora Liboro (Form 1), Flora Mesar (Form 2), Stella Kaputiu (Form 1), Frida Gathure (Form 1), and Jane Kajoki (Form 4).

The attack, about ten other girls were injured.

PAGE 10 – Col. 1

71 girls raped in St. Kizito tragedy

By IMANENE IMATHIU

Seventy-one girls were raped when rampaging boys raided their dormitories at the St. Kizito School in Meru District on Saturday night, medical authorities confirmed yesterday.

The five doctors attending to the victims who survived the raid in which 19 girls died told the Nation that the 71 girls were treated and discharged.

The doctors said the girls "were definitely raped."

Police are investigating the cause of the rampage but initial reports said it was occasioned by the girls' refusal to join in a strike action against the headmaster.

The students had the previous day been thrown out of a sports meet at another school for non-payment of activity fees. Back at the St. Kizito, the boys started plotting to stage a strike but the girls refused to join in, sources said.

On Saturday, the boys are said to have plunged the school into

darkness after short circuiting the electricity. They invaded the girls' dormitories shortly before midnight, sending them fleeing in terror into a small room. When police arrived at 5 am on Saturday, they found all the girls locked in. The door was jammed, 19 girls dead and 71 injured.

Yesterday, the Meru Medical Officer of Health, Dr Augustine Mwayiti, said statements to the

PAGE 10 – Col. 4

President Moi talks to some of the injured students at the Tigania Mission Hospital. They included Beatrice Kawira, Jacinta Karimi and Jane Mwenkoru. With them were the doctor in charge of the hospital, Dr Francis Kiithu, and the matron, Mrs Grace Mbaya. (Picture by JOSEPH ODIYO)

Ouko: Car boot 'had blood'

By GICHURU NJIHIA, CALEB ATEMI and MAKAU NIKO

A man supplied confidential information to the New Scotland Yard team investigating Dr Robert Ouko's death about how he cleaned his employer's car boot which had stains that indicated a great amount of blood had seeped in it.

The Commission of Inquiry into Dr Ouko's February 1990 death was also told yesterday that the Minister's younger brother, Mr Barrack Mbajah, was held in police custody for four

days, quizzed by the UK detectives and a search conducted at his Nairobi residence.

Senior Superintendent of Police Humphrey Kariuki said the information about the car's being cleaned of blood came from a letter received in Kisumu from Mombasa.

SSP Kariuki told the Commission that the letter was posted at Changamwe in Mombasa on March 3, last year, and was received by a nephew of Dr Ouko's, Mr Amos Agalo, on March 12.

The letter, which was written in Swahili, came through the Minister's Koru Post Office box.

the Commission heard.

"It was written by somebody who said that he was asked by his employer to clean the boot of a car which had blood stains, almost a debe of blood in that boot," SSP Kariuki told the Commission.

He said the writer of the letter was a man, but he could not remember his name. The letter was taken by the Yard's Detective Sergeant Sandy Sanderson and handed over to Detective Ken Lindsay, also of Scotland Yard.

The Commission heard, for the first time, that Det Supt John Troon secured authority to ex-

amine Dr Ouko's Kenya Commercial Bank Office Avenue, Nairobi account on March 19 last year.

The witness did not disclose the details of the probe.

About Dr Ouko's brother, the witness, who was at the heart of most of the Ouko investigations conducted by the Kenya Police and also assisted the British detectives, said Det Supt Troon wanted to interview Mr Mbajah on March 24, last year, but this was not possible because the latter was ill.

The matter was deferred until

PAGE 2 – Col. 1

Illustration 5. Daily Nation front page, 17 July 1991. "Death dormitory moves Moi to tears," by Irungu Ndirangu, and "71 girls raped in St. Kizito tragedy," by Imanene Imathiu, picture by Joseph Odiyo. Three survivors are named in this photograph of President Moi's visit to Tigania Mission Hospital.

Appendix A

List of St. Kizito Stories Analyzed

Headline	Author	Date	Page No.
Daily Nation			
Moi orders thorough investigation as . . . Rampaging boys leave 19 girls dead	Irungu Ndirangu, Imanene Imathiu, KNA•	7/15/91	1, 2
Meru tragedy: Boys' parents get ultimatum	N/A	7/16/91	1, 2
Morals were never so low in schools (ed.)	N/A	7/16/91	6
71 girls raped in St. Kizito tragedy	Imanene Imathiu•	7/17/91	1, 18
Death dormitory moves Moi to tears	Irungu Ndirangu•	7/17/91	1, 18
Leaders condemn girls' killing	Victor Nzuma, Joseph Olweny, Imanene Imathiu•	7/17/91	2
Team named to probe indiscipline in schools	Wamahiu Muya•	7/18/91	1, 2
St. Kizito girls' transfers ready	N/A	7/18/91	1, 2
Shops, schools shut as thousands mourn	Irungu Ndirangu•	7/19/91	1, 15
Hooliganism deplorable (letter)	A. Ndelwa Musyoka	7/19/91	7
Rape rampage was terrible (letter)	Edwin M. Mguru•	7/19/91	7
St. Kizito tragedy watchman charged	Imanene Imathiu•	7/20/91	1
Meru DC puts off transfer of girls	Imanene Imathiu•	7/20/91	1, 2
Doctors link Meru tragedy to stress	N/A	7/20/91	2
St. Kizito students suspended, 39 held	Imanene Imathiu•	7/22/91	1, 2

Headline	Author	Date	Page No.
Women want more posts	N/A	7/22/91	3
Society is to blame for rising school violence (editorial)	Wahome Mutahi•	7/22/91	6
Get rid of mixed schools (letter)	P. S. Wanjala•	7/22/91	7
An idea to ease the workload (letter)	J. Clifton•	7/22/91	7
This called for soul-searching (letter)	Gladys K. Mwiti*	7/22/91	7
Drink or drugs aren't to blame (letter)	Charles K. N. Ikuru•	7/22/91	7
Try to understand your students (letter)	Wanyax wa Chebbs	7/22/91	7
St. Kizito is society problem (letter)	Agnes Karanja*	7/22/91	7
Consider boys' psychology too	Mwaria ma Ndendwo	7/22/91	7
Kizito girls suffocated	Imanene Imathiu•	7/23/91	26
St. Kizito: President cautions newspapers	N/A	7/24/91	1
St. Kizito headteacher was "inexperienced"	N/A	7/24/91	28
Let's seek universal remedy (letter)	Gichingu Thuku	7/25/91	7
Girls from St. Kizito transferred	Imanene Imathiu•	7/25/91	32
Women to discuss child abuse	N/A	7/26/91	3
The 8-4-4 factor in schools' unrest (3 letters)	David K. Wang'ombe, David K. Maigiro, Mwangi Kanunda•	7/26/91	7
Find out the St. Kizito horror (letter)	Kaburi Franz•	7/26/91	7
Pray for Muge and St. Kizito girls—Yego	N/A	7/29/91	11
St. Kizito tragedy: 29 boys charged	Imanene Imathiu•	7/30/91	1, 2
Women to visit St. Kizito	N/A	7/31/91	3
Officer: Ten St. Kizito boys still in custody	N/A	7/31/91	32
Women call for family courts	N/A	8/1/91	3
Strokes for boys who scared girls	N/A	8/2/91	1, 2
Kakamega Kizito head summoned	N/A	8/3/91	3
Society is to blame (letter)	Peter Moll•	8/7/91	7
St. Kizito tragedy: Boy denies charges	N/A	8/7/91	28
Nine St. Kizito boys are freed by court	Imanene Imathiu•	8/8/91	28
Oyier: Get rid of mixed schools	N/A	8/13/91	4
30 Kizito boys "in thugs den"	Imanene Imathiu•	8/13/91	4
Service in memory of St. Kizito girls	Emman Omari•	8/14/91	3

Headline	Author	Date	Page No.
Court to visit Kizito schoolboys in prison	N/A	8/14/91	32
This violence should stop now	Martha Mbugguss*	8/14/91	8
Diocese urges 8-4-4 review	Michael Njuguna•	8/20/91	3
30 St. Kizito boys punished before trial—lawyers	Imanene Imathiu•	8/28/91	5
Form 4 Kizito boys recalled	Imanene Imathiu•	9/11/91	3
Kizito boys cannot be bonded—court	N/A	9/11/91	4
57 St. Kizito boys moved	Imanene Imathiu•	9/13/91	4
Kizito boys likely to flee, counsel says	N/A	9/14/91	3
43 St. Kizito boys report to Kangaru High School	N/A	9/18/91	4
Kizito boys sent to different schools	Imanene Imathiu•	9/20/91	4
St. Kizito boys' plea dismissed	N/A	9/21/91	28
St. Kizito boys are ill—lawyer	Imanene Imathiu•	10/10/91	32
St. Kizito boys allowed bond	N/A	10/17/91	28
No exam for 9 St. Kizito boys	N/A	10/19/91	4
New magistrate for Kizito case	N/A	12/3/91	5
St. Kizito girl: Boy tried to rape me	Imanene Imathiu•	12/4/91	16
Teacher helped remove Kizito dead	Imanene Imathiu•	12/4/91	20
St. Kizito: Nurse took body specimens	Imanene Imathiu•	12/5/91	4
Public sent out of St. Kizito hearing	Imanene Imathiu•	12/6/91	5
Kizito boys, girls "used to misbehave"	Imanene Imathiu•	12/10/91	24
Kizito boys wanted to see "their wives"	Imanene Imathiu•	12/11/91	24
Kizito students had grievances	Imanene Imathiu•	12/12/91	14
Kizito students threatened to kill headmaster	Imanene Imathiu•	12/13/91	32
St. Kizito: KNUT protests sacking	Imanene Imathiu•	12/14/91	28
St. Kizito dormitory "built on haunted site"	Imanene Imathiu•	12/17/91	20
Court to visit St. Kizito today	N/A	12/19/91	5
St. Kizito: All the boys misbehaved, court told	N/A	12/21/91	16
Meru starts phasing out mixed schools . . .	Imanene Imathiu•	12/26/91	14
1991 marred by St. Kizito and riots	N/A	1/2/92	12
Watchmen "padlocked" Kizito girls' dormitory	N/A	1/8/92	15
Kizito 15 have case to answer	Imanene Imathiu•	1/11/92	4

Headline	Author	Date	Page No.
Second Kizito hearing deferred	Imanene Imathiu, Njoroge wa Karuri•	2/18/92	13
4 St. Kizito boys jailed for manslaughter	Imanene Imathiu•	2/19/92	1, 6
Order on St. Kizito boys	KNA	3/5/92	23
St. Kizito: Four boys jailed	KNA	3/18/92	5
8 St. Kizito boys freed	N/A	3/26/92	2
Former prefect at St. Kizito testifies	Imanene Imathiu•	4/3/92	13
St. Kizito boys guilty	N/A	4/29/92	2
St. Kizito: "Funds not submitted"	N/A	5/19/92	5
Girls transferred for safety	Joe Ombuor•	5/30/92	14
Prayers for rape victims proposed	N/A	7/11/92	5
St. Kizito tragedy memorial service	N/A	7/13/92	1
St. Kizito tragedy marked in city	Sheila Wambui*	7/15/92	4
St. Kizito boys "successfully rehabilitated"	N/A	10/21/92	20

The Sunday Nation

Headline	Author	Date	Page No.
Kizito: 20 more boys arrested	Imanene Imathiu•	7/21/91	1, 2
Why strikes and St. Kizito tragedy had to happen	Wamahiu Muya•	7/21/91	VII, X, XV
A country grapples with the aftermath of gross student indiscipline . . . Could this tragedy have been averted?	Irungu Ndirangu•	7/21/91	VIII–IX
Kenyans react angrily as they urge for a permanent solution	Jane Some, Marianne King 'Ori, James Wahome*	7/21/91	VII-IX
Kizito: The worst of a worsening situation	Wamahiu Muya•	7/21/91	X
Ministry should act promptly over children	Mkanju•	7/21/91	XII
Kamotho decries lack of discipline	Odhiambo-Oriale•	7/21/91	21
Parents appeal for girl students' security	Peter Angwenyi•	8/4/91	5
Rape: Why the apathy?	Rasna Warah*	8/4/91	VIII
Kizito: Kanu women call for end to speculation	N/A	8/4/91	20
Kizito victims' memorial date set	David Rogoncho•	8/11/91	5
Why we have student unrest (letter)	Ignatius Mwenda Ngore•	8/25/91	10
In sexism, women are their own worst enemies	Rasna Warah*	9/22/91	6
St. Kizito boys' case to begin	Imanene Imathiu•	12/1/91	20

Headline	Author	Date	Page No.
Build more schools for girls (letter)	Otiento C. O. Jaseme•	12/1/91	10
Kizito tragedy our creation—lawyer	N/A	2/23/92	4
Officer cites "Kizito jealousy"	Imanene Imathiu•	5/17/92	5
St. Kizito: A Kenyan nightmare that won't go away/Victims sentenced to a lifetime of living with pain (2 stories)	Ngugi wa Mbugua•	6/21/92	8–9
Burying memory of night of madness	Christine Mpaka*	7/26/92	5

The Standard

Rampaging students flee after incident . . . 19 girls killed in rape ordeal	Xavier Lugaga, Victor Nzomo•	7/15/91	1, 2
Rampaging boys hide in bush	N/A	7/16/91	1, 13
The victims	N/A	7/16/91	1
Moi to visit school	Ngumo wa Kuria•	7/16/91	1, 13
Why this beastly student behavior? (editorial)	N/A	7/16/91	8
Moi sees "death chamber" horrors	N/A	7/17/91	1, 13
Knut calls for end to mixed boarding schools	Ngumo wa Kuria•	7/17/91	3
Kizito: Students now go back	N/A	7/17/91	3
St. Kizito boys were not alone, claims MP	Francis Muroki, Amos Marenya, John Kiama•	7/18/91	2
Police act as boys scare girls' school	N/A	7/18/91	8
Ordeal at Kizito	Raphael Kahaso•	7/18/91	20
Tragedy that shocked all	Raphael Kahaso•	7/18/91	21
How the calamity started	Xavier Lugaga•	7/18/91	21
An example of violence against women	Oketch Kendo•	7/18/91	21
Reconsider Kizito girls' transfer —Moi	N/A	7/19/91	1, 12
Headmaster and his deputy interdicted at . . . St. Kizito: 18 boys arrested over riot	Victor Nzomo•	7/20/91	1, 2
Riots: Time for action is now (opinion)	Gladys K. Mwitti*	7/20/91	II
School violence	Athanas Tuiyot•	7/20/91	II, III
Dialogue is the answer (opinion)	N/A	7/20/91	III
39 riotous students arrested . . . 265 St. Kizito's boys suspended	Victor Nzomo•	7/22/91	1, 2
Adults "poor role models"	KNA	7/22/91	3

Headline	Author	Date	Page No.
Don't exploit women—nuns	Enock Anjili•	7/22/91	14
Kizito girls recalled	N/A	7/23/91	5
Fingerprints of Kizito schoolboys recorded	N/A	7/24/91	5
Girls should remain at St. Kizito (letter)	Mrs. Margaret Njoroge*	7/24/91	9
President cautions papers over Kizito	N/A	7/24/91	13
Kizito girls transferred	Victor Nzomo•	7/25/91	1, 15
Students deny 19 separate charges . . . St. Kizito tragedy: 29 boys in court	Victor Nzomo•	7/30/91	1, 12
Use chaplains for moral uprightness (letter)	S. Moses Smith•	7/31/91	9
Parents are to blame	N/A	7/31/91	9
St. Kizito: 10 still held	Victor Nzomo•	7/31/91	14
Women in plea over violence	Kihu Irimu•	8/1/91	4
Six picked up at another St. Kizito	Patrick Wakhisi•	8/2/91	4
Cane for eighteen bullies	KNA	8/2/91	5
Another St. Kizito student on manslaughter charge	Victor Nzomo•	8/7/91	4
Kenyan women are angry	Kidji Nduku*	8/7/91	17, 20
St. Kizito: 9 boys bonded to keep peace	Victor Nzomo•	8/8/91	1
Dicipline team tours St. Kizito	N/A	8/9/91	5
Exercise care over TV screening of obscene viewing of youth (letters)	Nicholas P. Kariuki•	8/9/91	9
Kizito: Plea for bail rejected	Victor Nzomo•	8/14/91	2
Riots: The jobs factor	Githuku Gacheru•	8/14/91	3
St. Kizito girls are remembered	N/A	8/15/91	5
Order to school heads timely (editorial)	N/A	8/15/91	8
Riots caused by heads at schools, team told	Ngomo wa Kuria•	8/20/91	5
St. Kizito incident calls for revision of education policy (letter)	Masoud Salim Mazrui•	8/20/91	9
3 St. Kizito guards out on bond	Victor Nzomo•	8/23/91	4
8-4-4 expensive for parents	N/A	8/24/91	5
St. Kizito: Eight lawyers reject	Victor Nzomo•	8/28/91	2
St. Kizito: Court to ascertain boys' ages	Victor Nzomo•	9/11/91	4
St. Kizito students moved to Kangaru	Victor Nzomo•	9/13/91	13
State wants St. Kizito boys in custody for security	Victor Nzomo•	9/14/91	4

Headline	Author	Date	Page No.
43 Kizito boys in Kangaru	KNA	9/19/91	13
218 St. Kizito students transferred	Victor Nzomo•	9/20/91	3
St. Kizito: Bail bid fails	N/A	9/21/91	4
St. Kizito: Now students allowed bond	Victor Nzomo•	10/17/91	4
School changes its name	KNA	11/21/91	3
St. Kizito girl student recalls night of ordeal	Victor Nzomo•	12/4/91	2
Kizito: Tigania matron testifies	Victor Nzomo•	12/5/91	4
Court is cleared for rape evidence	Victor Nzomo•	12/6/91	4
St. Kizito: Mischief alleged	N/A	12/10/91	4
Kizito headmaster tells of death threats	Victor Nzomo•	12/13/91	4
St. Kizito: 4 girls had sex, court told	N/A	1/11/92	3
St. Kizito case: Ruling date set	N/A	1/18/92	5
Four St. Kizito boys jailed for four years	Victor Nzomo•	2/19/92	1, 2
Application rejected	N/A	3/4/92	4
Kizito boys get 16 years	N/A	3/18/92	12
Two St. Kizito boys guilty, 13 acquitted	Victor Nzomo•	4/29/92	13
Rape: Prayers planned	N/A	6/1/92	5
Mass said in memory of St. Kizito's deceased	N/A	7/15/92	3

The Sunday Standard

Headline	Author	Date	Page No.
Kizito tragedy: President's decision wins the day (editorial)	N/A	7/21/91	8
After St. Kizito a bonfire of our pride (TV & radio review)	John Kariuki•	7/21/91	12
St. Kizito: Students declared martyrs (TV & radio review)	John Kariuki•	7/28/91	12
St. Kizito: NGO to help 22 girls	Victor Nzomo•	8/4/91	2
MYWO call for end to violence against women	Alphonse Mung'ahu•	8/11/91	3
Women's organisation hits at Leitich over rape utterances	N/A	9/15/91	3
Women's issues: the time for action is now (editorial)	N/A	9/29/91	8
School discipline begins at home (editorial)	N/A	11/3/91	8
Are women responsible for rape (opinion)	Rasna Warah*	5/3/92	2

Headline	Author	Date	Page No.
St. Kizito prayers today	N/A	7/12/92	4

Kenya Times

Headline	Author	Date	Page No.
19 girls killed in school rape	Alex Riithi•	7/15/91	1, 2
Meru villagers mourn their dead	Murigi Macharia•	7/16/91	1, 2
After Meru co-education tragedy . . . Moi moves to protect girls	Murigi Macharia, Alex Riithi, KNA•	7/17/91	1, 18
Kizito rape probe opens . . . Team to report to Moi in 3 months	N/A	7/18/91	1, 2
Aringo: Plotters responsible for children's riots	Mwicigi Njoroge•	7/18/91	1, 2
Night of horror revisited	Murigi Macharia•	7/18/91	1, 15
St. Kizito tragedy: Biwott hails Moi	N/A	7/18/91	5
Lessons from Kizito (editorial)	Robert Otani•	7/18/91	6
Leave Kizito girls alone, orders Moi	Murigi Macharia, Julia Gichuhi*	7/19/91	1, 2
Kizito boys are like dogs, Karauri	Alex Riithi•	7/19/91	3
Watchman charged in Kizito rape, death cases	Alex Riithi•	7/20/91	1, 2
Kizito: Parents throng to school	Alex Riithi•	7/20/91	2
Letters dispatched from TSC . . . Kizito head interdicted	Alex Riithi•	7/20/91	2
Kizito incident leaves the republic in state of shock	Charles Kulundu•	7/20/91	13
Seeking the roots of students' indiscipline	Mwicigi Njoroge•	7/20/91	18
School murder, rape in focus	Bobby Kiama•	7/20/91	18, 19
St. Kizito and the Pharisees in the Christian church (ed.)	Philip Ochieng•	7/22/91	1, 6–7
Now rape murder school is shut	Alex Riithi, Aggreg Ouma•	7/22/91	1, 2
Bishop calls for St. Kizito closure	Michael Oongo•	7/22/91	4
Report to DC, Kizito girls told	Alex Riithi•	7/23/91	2
Discipline: PC appeals to parents	N/A	7/23/91	4
Another St. Kizito shocker, Questions that weren't answered	Alex Riithi•	7/24/91	1, 7
Kizito: Moi warns papers . . . Don't use tragedy to incite schools	Murigi Macharia, KNA•	7/24/91	2

Headline	Author	Date	Page No.
It's a deserted, desolate Kizito	Alex Riithi•	7/24/91	4
Now St. Kizito girls join other schools	Alex Riithi•	7/25/91	3
Stop other Kizito tragedies (3 letters)	Kaburi Franz, Margaret Njoroge, S. Wafala*	7/29/91	7
29 Kizito boys deny rape, other charges	Alex Riithi•	7/30/91	1, 2
Kizito phobia sweeps schools	Alex Riithi•	7/31/91	3
Kizito: Society should instil morality in youth	Pio Ciampa, S.J.	7/31/91	7
Family violence: women's bodies take up the cudgel	Cecilia Kamau*	8/1/91	1, 2
Violence: women appeal to government	Charles Kulundu•	8/3/91	15
Catholics must learn to fight evil (letter)	Robin Taabu•	8/6/91	7
"St. Kizito boys will not sit for exams"	Mwicigi Njoroge•	8/8/91	2
St. Kizito: Nine boys bonded	Alex Riithi•	8/8/91	3
Student unrest: Omido advises headteachers	KNA	8/13/91	4
St. Kizito: Lawyers demand boys' bond	N/A	8/13/91	12
Memorial for Kizito girls held	N/A	8/14/91	2
Kizito court petitioned	N/A	8/14/91	4
Befitting memorial for St. Kizito girls	Cecilia Kamau*	8/15/91	6
St. Kizito: We should encourage counselling, discipline in schools (letter)	Willis Tsuma Musungu•	8/16/91	7
Mixed schools now appear untenable	Mwicigi Njoroge•	8/17/91	21
Headmasters, stop acting like tyrants	N/A	8/19/91	1, 6
St. Kizito: Watchmen bonded	KNA	8/23/91	5
30 St. Kizito boys denied bail	Alex Riithi•	8/28/91	12
Don't abolish mixed schools (opinion)	D. J. Ndegwah wa Nyamburah•	9/5/91	7
Body vows to fight for rights of women	N/A	9/6/91	3
Dreadful human rights violation	Philip Ochieng•	9/11/91	1, 6, 12
St. Kizito boys to do exams at Kangaru	Alex Riithi•	9/13/91	5
St. Kizito: Date for plea set	N/A	9/14/91	2
St. Kizito students to be shifted	Alex Riithi•	9/18/91	5
Kizito boys released on bond	Alex Riithi•	10/17/91	2
Headgirl testifies in Kizito rape case	Alex Riithi•	12/4/91	12

Headline	Author	Date	Page No.
St. Kizito: Matron testifies	Alex Riithi•	12/5/91	13
The year in review	N/A	12/27/91	20
Warrant for St. Kizito boy	KNA	1/2/92	5
St. Kizito boys have a case to answer	Alex Riithi•	1/11/92	3
St. Kizito case put off again	N/A	2/18/92	12
Four St. Kizito boys imprisoned	Alex Riithi•	2/19/92	1, 3
St. Kizito revisited	Alex Riithi•	4/8/92	14, 15
Otunga's rape quip slammed	N/A	4/21/92	2
Kizito memorial planned	N/A	7/11/92	4

The Sunday Times

Headline	Author	Date	Page No.
Kizito: Are we qualified to talk of indiscipline? (opinion)	Mugambi Karanja•	7/21/91	6, 7
Who were behind the St. Kizito tragedy (letter)	Schamallah Momo•	7/28/91	7
School riots: Women caution against talk	KNA	8/4/91	3
Female breasts obscene, says body	N/A	8/18/91	2
Mixed schools should be abolished (letter)	Masoud Salim Mazrui•	8/25/91	7
Women's passivity to blame for their woes	Dr. Maria Nzomo*	9/8/91	12, 29
Women rap MP over rape story	N/A	9/15/91	4
Boys chased away after rape threat	Maurice Masika, Michael Oongo•	10/20/91	3

Weekly Review

Headline	Author	Date	Page No.
Letter from the editor	Hilary Ng'weno•	7/19/91	1
The Meru tragedy	N/A	7/19/91	5–13
Kizito tragedy (letter)	Lee Muthoga•	7/26/91	2
Making the punishment fit the crime	N/A	7/26/91	14–16
Manslaughter charges in Kizito case	N/A	8/2/91	8
Kizito tragedy (letter)	Ken Imathiu•	8/2/91	2
St. Kizito (letter)	Ignatius Mwenda Ngore•	8/9/91	2
St. Kizito (letter)	"Another Kenyan Scribe"	8/9/91	2
St. Kizito (letter)	Adulrahman Mwabili•	8/9/91	3
St. Kizito (letter)	Mathew Kibe•	8/9/91	3

Headline	Author	Date	Page No.
Sexism in Kenya: The Woman's Lot is Not a Happy One	N/A	8/9/91	4–20
Women's "right to say no"'	R. M. Kahumbu	8/23/91	2
Nine Kizito boys are bonded	N/A	8/23/91	13–14
Sexism (letter)	Mutahi P. T. M.•	9/6/91	2
Letter from the editor	Hilary Ng'weno•	9/13/91	1
Men and women (letter)	Frank N. Thuranira•	9/13/91	2
Men and women (letter)	N/A	9/13/91	2
Taking the bull by the horns	N/A	9/13/91	15–18
Cleaning up after St. Kizito	N/A	9/20/91	11
Olive branch	N/A	10/11/91	7–11
1991: Rape and death in Meru	N/A	12/20/91	37
Strategies to bolster women	N/A	2/28/92	16–17
A year later: Taking stock	N/A	7/17/92	23-24

International Reports (NEXIS)

Headline	Author	Date	Page No.
19 school girls die after rape ordeal (AFP)	N/A	7/14/91	
Nineteen Kenyan schoolgirls killed in dormitory attack (Reuters)	N/A	7/14/91	
Gang rape leaves 19 Kenyan school girls dead, 75 injured (AFP)	N/A	7/15/91	
19 schoolgirls killed (*Newsday*)	N/A	7/15/91	14
Boys at Kenya school rape girls, killing 19 (NY Times Co., *NY Times*)	N/A	7/15/91	A3
19 Kenyan girls killed in dorm attack (*Orlando Sentinal Tribune*)	N/A	7/15/91	A6
Kenyan school closed after 19 girls die in dormitory raid (Reuters)	Manoah Esipisu•	7/15/91	
Kurdish leader says agreement is near (world news brief) (*St. Petersburg Times*)	N/A	7/15/91	6A
Croatian militia retakes four Serbian-held villages (world news brief) (*USA Today*)	N/A	7/15/91	4A
Boys raid girls' dorm; many raped, 19 die (*Washington Times*)	N/A	7/15/91	A2
School massacre (*The Independent*)	N/A	7/15/91	10

Headline	Author	Date	Page No.
19 Kenyan girls die in teen dorm attack (*Chicago Tribune*)	N/A	7/15/91	10
Kenya's social tensions highlighted by schoolgirl killings (AFP)	David Chazan•	7/16/91	
Kenya's president visits "death chamber" (Reuters)	Manoah Esipisu•	7/16/91	
KGB agent says it's tough to spy in U.S. (world news brief) (*Atlanta Journal and Constitution*)	N/A	7/16/91	A6
School is shut after 19 deaths (*The Independent*)	N/A	7/16/91	10
19 killed in school rampage in Kenya (*Courier-Journal*)	N/A	7/16/91	4A
Kenyan minister blames drink, drugs for school disaster (Reuters)	Manoah Esipisu•	7/17/91	
Kenya: student riots shake up nation (Inter Press Service)	Horace Awori•	7/17/91	
Moi pledge (*The Independent*)	N/A	7/17/91	10
Team named to investigate indiscipline in Kenyan schools (Xinhua General News Service)	N/A	7/18/91	
Kenyan police say arrests completed at murder school (Reuters)	Manoah Esipisu•	7/22/91	
Death and rape at school force Kenya to look at education crisis (Reuters)	Manoah Esipisu•	7/22/91	
Officials suspend all boys in Kenyan rape and murder school (Reuters)	N/A	7/22/91	
Teens held in classmates' killings (*St. Louis Post-Dispatch*)	N/A	7/22/91	7A
More S. Africa aid to Inkatha disclosed (world news brief) (*St. Petersburg Times*)	N/A	7/22/91	7A
38 Kenyan schoolboys held in dorm deaths (*Washington Times*)	N/A	7/22/91	A2
Kenya closes troublesome school indefinitely (Xinhua General News Service)	N/A	7/22/91	
39 students arrested, 265 suspended in school killings (AFP)	N/A	7/22/91	
39 boys held in Kenya after dormitory rampage (Pacific Press Ltd., *Vancouver Sun*)	N/A	7/23/91	
39 boys arrested in dorm rampage (*The Ottawa Citizen*)	N/A	7/23/91	

Headline	Author	Date	Page No.
39 boys arrested after 19 girls die in attack at Kenya boarding school (Times-Mirror Co., *LA Times*)	N/A	7/23/91	A4
Rape was common at Kenyan school before tragedy: headmaster (AFP)	N/A	7/24/91	
Kenyans do some soul-searching after the rape of 71 schoolgirls (NY Times Co., *NY Times*)	Jane Perlez*	7/29/91	A1
29 Kenyan students charged with manslaughter in school raid (Reuters)	N/A	7/29/91	
Kenyan riot boys in court (Times Newspaper Ltd., *The Times*)	N/A	7/30/91	
Cavemen try taking women back in time: The Stone Age (*Newsday*)	Sheryl McCarthy*	7/31/91	8
The evil men do to women in Kenya (*NY Times*)	Jane Perlez*	8/4/91	A4
Horrified Kenya looks inward (*Philadephia Inquirer*)	Timothy Dwyer•	8/11/91	A1
A night of madness (*Time* magazine)	N/A	8/12/91	43
Perspectives (*Newsweek*)	N/A	8/12/91	15
School attack inspires action by women of Kenya (*Toronto Star*)	N/A	8/12/91	F1
Vigil for Kenyan girls (Times-Mirror Co., *LA Times*)	N/A	8/13/91	1
Kenyan court refused bail to 30 boys charged with manslaughter (Reuters)	N/A	8/13/91	
Behind Kenya's push for multiparty reform (Christian Science Publishing Society, *Christian Science Monitor*)	Robert M. Press•	8/14/91	4
Kenya court rejects bail in school tragedy (*Washington Times*)	N/A	8/14/91	A2
No bail for 30 teens accused of pillaging Kenya school (*Chicago Tribune*)	N/A	8/14/91	4
Kenyans haunted by girls' deaths (*Chicago Tribune*)	Timothy Dwyer•	8/18/91	25
Mass rape at boarding school (Facts on File World News Digest)	N/A	8/22/91	535
Currents, From Kenya (*Newsday*)	N/A	9/1/91	50
School attack inspires action by women of Kenya (*Toronto Star*)	Michele Landsberg*	10/12/91	F1

Headline	Author	Date	Page No.
NOW chapter issues "turkey of the year" awards (UPI)	N/A	11/25/91	
When women are prey; around the world, rape is commonplace and the victims can't fight back (*Washington Post*)	Lori Heise*	12/8/91	C1
Four Kenyan youths jailed for gang rape that killed 19 girls (AFP)	N/A	2/19/92	
10 Kenya students guilty in girls' deaths (*Washington Times*)	N/A	2/20/92	A2
African students convicted in riot deaths of 19 coeds (*Jet*)	N/A	3/9/92	25
Boys cleared in killing Kenya schoolgirls (Reuters)	N/A	3/26/92	
Eight Kenyan youths acquitted of gang rape that killed 19 girls (AFP)	N/A	3/26/92	
Kenya acquittals (*The Independent*)	N/A	3/27/92	10
Kenya: New name, but old values still haunt Kenya's school of infamy (*The Age*, Melbourne, from Reuters text)	James Schofield•	7/13/92	

Appendix A lists all stories about St. Kizito analyzed in the Kenyan press and in the international press for the year following the crime: from July 14, 1991 through July of 1992, inclusive of anniversary stories (see also Chapter 2 for a description of the sample). The Appendix does not include press stories cited in the endnotes that do not refer to St. Kizito and/or were published after July of 1992. The acronym "N/A" means no known author, as the story has no byline. The acronym "KNA" means Kenya News Agency authorship. Asterisks (*) indicate at least one known female reporter, based on the author's personal knowledge or consultations with Kenyan informants. Dots (•) indicate male reporters.

Appendix B

Another St. Kizito Shocker:
Questions that weren't answered
by Alex Riithi

Kenya Times, 24 July 1991, pp. 1, 7

The rape of schoolgirls by their male colleagues has been a common occurrence at St. Kizito Mixed Secondary School in Tigania, Meru, *Kenya Times* investigations have revealed.

The school's headmaster, Mr. James Laibuni told me: "In the past, the boys would scare the girls, out of their dormitories and in the process they would get hold of them and drag them to the bush where they would 'do their thing' and the matter would end there, with the students going back to their respective dormitories."

But on the night of Saturday, July 13, the matter didn't end that "normally." In an incident that has shocked the world, 19 of the girl students died, 71 raped and scores more injured. Yet, incredibly, members of the local community surrounding the school say they didn't think there was anything unusual about the screams and cries of agony from the girl students as their male colleagues went on their orgy of killing and destruction that night.

"I believe none of the boys intended to kill," headmaster Laibuni, now interdicted, told me. "This must have been a joke turned nasty. The boys just wanted to have a nice time with their girls and this has been the case whenever there were disturbances in the school in the past."

Some joke. Some past. But even more shocking is the attitude of the local community. Neither the screams of terror nor the groans of girls dying in the very prime of their lives moved the villagers living around St. Kizito School out of their beds. They had heard it all before. They simply turned over and went back to sleep. If there was any trouble at the school, that was the school administration's baby, reasoned the school's neighbours, including those at the adjacent Muiri Market.

Mrs. Pierina Ituri said: "We heard the noise all right, but we have been hearing this kind of noise from the school every year so we never thought anything could be seriously wrong." Mrs. Ituri, whose home is just a few metres from the school, said any time there has been such noise in the past they would wake up and find that "there was nothing serious but only the raping of the girls by the boys."

A man who lives at Muiri Market, Mr. Mung'atia, said he had heard the noise too but assumed the matter was "simple" as it was "usually" an affair between the boys and the girls whenever they heard such noise in the past.

The villagers' attitude towards rape was clear—that it was normal so long as it was boys versus "their" girls—and this prompted me to talk to the now interdicted school headmaster, Laibuni, whose disposition towards sexual behaviour was even more explicit.

Mr. Laibuni, who was in the school compound for the better part of the six-day screening exercise until he received an interdiction letter last Thursday, was composed throughout and very willing to talk to all, including the Press and the horde of security personnel deployed at the school since that fateful Saturday night.

This *laissez-faire* attitude towards sex was also exemplified by the explanation of the tragedy by the school's deputy headmistress, Mrs. Joyce Kithira, who told President Moi when he visited the school: "The boys never meant any harm against the girls. They just wanted to rape."

With the foregoing, it is clear that teachers and the community have never seen anything wrong with rape. For example, one old man had this to say regarding rape: "In our days whenever I did anything like this, and it was reported to my parents, my mother used to get very happy for this is how she knew in me she had a man in the making—but nowadays you do it and you are rushed to court."

But as we delve into this incident that still remains a nightmare for most of the girls who survived the ordeal there are many questions that cry loudly for answers. For instance:

1. Were the school administration and the local administration aware of any build-up of tension among the boys or was there no tension because the boys' intention was just to rape and not to kill, as some teachers and villagers put it?

2. There was a bhang smoking and *chang'aa* drinking den called Shimo-la-Tewa just next to the school which was shown to the President by the chief inspector of schools, Mr. Tom Sitima; was the school administration aware of this and if so why was drug addiction allowed to continue ruining the boys?

My investigations revealed that the boys and girls of St. Kizito had had an outing that Saturday and there was nothing apparent in the offing to indicate that they would turn against their sisters later that night. All those interviewed, including the headmaster, insisted that there was no tension in the school but it beats logic how a struggle leading to the death of as high as number 19 in a school would ensue without bitterness on the part of the assailants.

All the beds, clothes, boxes and other personal effects in the Batian dormitory, otherwise now known as the "death chamber," were in a total mess—twisted metal and all. This could not have happened without a major struggle in the chamber where the 19 bodies of the girls plus the injured were found by the police at 3:00 AM on Sunday. The boys were also said to have used torches in identifying the girls they wanted for the purpose of rape: How then did such a disarray occur?

Much as the school administration may deny that there was tension in the school, there were revealing facts pointing to this factor. The headmaster had a few months earlier received several threatening letters, and he himself confirmed finding a note under his door on the morning of the same Saturday. In the note, the students had complained about what they termed exaggerated fees balances.

The letter went thus, according to Mr. Laibuni: "Sir, you are spending sleepless nights because of our fees balances but these balances are wrong. The clerks gave you wrong figures and you budget on them. Try to find out from us in class. We also have too many workers in the school: six cooks, one cateress, four groundsmen, an office messenger and three watchmen."

Mr. Laibuni almost admits that there was prevailing tension when he says: "I held an impromptu meeting with the prefects on realising that there was a problem."

But Mr. Laibuni's problems could not have been solved by his prefects, some of whom, though it is too early to comment, were among those mentioned by some girls as having been involved in the ghastly attack. And these included the school captain, Joshua Njate, and his deputy, Mbaya Stephen, who are already in police custody.

Another thing that stands out clearly about the school is that there is an apparent general atmosphere of laziness. The compound is quite small but with no grass cut while the number of buildings (that would require clearing) is also small, giving the impression that over the weekend or during the weekdays students had nothing else to do on leaving classes.

Maybe because of idleness or laxity on the part of the administration, there has been a tendency by the boys to go out smoking or drinking in the nearby huts that literally surround the school or in the bush on the other end of the institution. Mr. Laibuni said there were some people who were peddling bhang and even Mandrax tablets to the school but could not explain why he had not stamped this out.

The headmaster even explained to the newsmen that the peddler was selling two tablets of Mandrax at Sh10 and that a single tablet of the drug, once taken, had the effect of 10 Tusker beer bottles. This being the case, maybe the boys "went on their normal rape rampage" but with most of them having had their sensibility taken away by drugs and *chang'aa*, they never realised that they were actually using extreme force that would eventually consign 19 of their female colleagues to an early grave. And then they raped 71 girls before sobering up and melting into the thin air that bloody Sunday morning.

The boys left the school in an orderly manner through an opening in the barbed wire next to the death chamber, in a single file, which leaves one wondering why even with bhang or whatever else they had taken they never panicked on learning about what they had done, or injured themselves during their flight to safety.

No wonder, even during the interrogation exercise which took top security officers six days they seemed not to care about what they had done at the school. Some were even rude to security officers as the officers inspected their belongings at the school.

This gave me the impression that the boys were probably exemplifying the surrounding community's "toughness"—a thing taught at circumcision: that one has to be hard and tough and ready to fight when belittled or slighted, etc. On circumcision boys are told: "You are now a DC (district commissioner)." The implication in this simple peasant community is that a boy-turned-man can now do pretty much whatever he pleases.

A worker at the school, Miss Mercy Tharamba, said the boys had a list of girls who had slighted them by befriending men from outside the school. These marked girls were Viola Karambu, Faith Mithika, Jane Karambu, Jane Karoki and Flora Rimboro. According to her, the boys had vowed to punish these girls even by death for, by their behaviour, the girls had overlooked the issue that the boys were like the implied all-powerful DC—they were also circumcised just like, those men the girls befriended. All the five girls died during the rape orgy.

By their defiance—which was obvious even after the murderous adventure—were the boys feeling on top of the world for being "real men" by doing what many have not done during their

school life—killing and raping helpless girls? When he re-
searched into and compiled a report on murders in Meru, a prac-
tising criminologist, Mr. Francis Machira Apollos, the District
Probation Officer, said Tigania, where the incident occurred, is
one of the areas in Meru where there is a subculture of violence
brought about mainly by the rigid traditions that are still deep
rooted, especially as far as circumcision is concerned. These traditions, furthermore, reinforce attitudes that perpetuate the subjugation of women, glorify male chauvinism and promote male
violence against women.

Listen to this conversation between a police officer and a man
from the area who was once taken into custody after attempting
to kill another man.

Policeman: You stabbed that man and he almost died.

Response: What do you mean he almost died? Can you release
me to go and kill that bastard if he is not already dead?

During my investigations, I concluded that if the cultural attitudes of the area are not what directly and indirectly led to the
rape and murder, then there must have been a well-organised
syndicate, probably under oath, to perpetrate the cruel and
beastly act. And should this have been the case then the issue of
outsiders being involved cannot be ruled out and this is given
credence by the fact that even after learning of the deaths no vil-
lager assisted in the arrest of boys, all of whom, I established,
were in school uniform as they fled.

Although a senior security officer whom the *Kenya Times* interviewed said it would have been difficult to arrest the boys after
they had gone to their homes—because that would have meant
going to 304 homes searching for them—the public expected
those living near the school to have arrested at least a few considering the magnitude of the ordeal. But this was not the case
and, apart from the three boys who were found cowering in their
dormitory (and these were sick and could not run away, according to security sources), all the rest fled to their homes. It was
not until Tuesday, after the Meru DC, Mr. Peter Saisi, had issued
an ultimatum for them to come back to school, that the boys
started pouring in.

The security officer further said the Chief Inspector of Schools, Mr. Sitima, had got his information about Shimo-la-Tewa, the bhang and *chang'aa* den, from the school administration, who had apparently done nothing about the situation, leaving the drug abuse and addiction to degenerate to uncontrollable proportions.

Another peculiar thing about the raid is the style used by the boys, and/or their accessories, if any. They made sure there were no lights or functioning telephones in the school and in the neighbourhood. At the St. Kizito Catholic Mission and Tigania Hospital, telephone facilities were also severed before the ugly incident was perpetrated.

It was also odd how the three watchmen at the school never did much to contain the situation but just fled when threatened by the boys. Kanake, one of the night guards, said he and his colleagues merely went to check whatever was happening when the boys started rioting and that once being pelted with stones by the unruly mob "we fled and went to report at the police station," but, surprisingly, the watchmen, whose job it is to keep security and ensure thugs are kept at bay, were beaten in this by some two teachers who had already arrived at the Tigania Police Station by the time the watchmen arrived there.

Claims by the watchmen that they were beaten and that they received injuries were not true as I personally saw them before they talked to the Kenya Broadcasting Corporation team, where they become excited on seeing the mike and exaggerated things with one saying: "I was beaten here . . . here . . . here . . . here . . ." (all the while pointing at various parts of his body just for the camera). Earlier, the same people had said they never received any injuries and only one of them had shown newsmen an extremely minor scratch on the upper side of his middle finger.

One agrees that the watchmen had a duty to go reporting to the police but should this have happened when some teachers had already undertaken to do so? Or was there no co-ordination between the watchmen and the teachers? I thought the first thing the teachers would have done before proceeding to the police station (where they are said to have preceded the watchmen) was to find out from the watchmen how the situation was. If this had happened it is common knowledge that the watchmen would not have fled and later coined the cock-and-bull story that they went reporting. And even if this had happened, then they should not have left the school at the total mercy of the unruly boys who had already stormed the girls' dormitory by the time of their (watchmen's flight).

As we mourn the departed souls of the 19 young girls who would have given a hand in nation building, what happened at St. Kizito should serve as a pointer to self-evaluation by all in the Kenyan society. The Government should be more thorough in the recruitment of those who head institutions and never hesitate to do away with deadwood for a repeat of such an incident would be an unbearable shame.

Appendix C

Feminist Voices: Story Samples

An example of violence against women
by Oketch Kendo
The Standard, 18 July 1991, p. 21

At this very moment 19 girls lie dead. Massacred by marauding men. Several others are in hospital recovering from the trauma they will never be able to forget. More than 19 homes are in mourning. The nation is stupefied by an event so disturbing, struggling to come to terms with events that took place on Saturday night. An experience so nightmarish, a crime so horrendous and an act so disarming.

Why did these girls have to die? What was their crime? While the country is grappling with the intensity of this despicable act, theories around the incident remain vague and incomprehensible.

We are told the girls refused to join the boys in a strike against their headmaster. We are told they were enraged by a missed sporting activity. The act has been dismissed as an act of hooliganism, of indiscipline gone berserk.

Poor leadership and lack of dialogue have been adduced as

explanations for a crime so barbaric. Probe has been appointed and head teachers and their assistants have been ordered to stay in schools.

Condolences have been sent and tears of repulsion have been shed. But is this act, this base massacre just another case of indiscipline by wayward pupils? Is it like a case of university students burning other people's cars?:

Or, is it just another case of habitual insanity in one another school?—part of a strike culture eating our educational institutions?

The Kizito Massacre stands out as different in several respects. The problem is deeper than many of us are inclined to believe.

Certain questions have got to be asked and the malaise has got to be stared in the face:

How come those who died are all girls? Did all boy students join the strike? If these boys had the audacity to force several girls into a strike, why didn't they face the headmaster as a body? Were the girls strong enough to undermine their decision to strike? Why did they rape and why did they cause death to a lot so hapless and innocent? Need we ask more questions? Where were the police?

The victims were all women. Cowed. Raped. Beaten and killed or left for dead. They are dead at the hands of bullish men masquerading as students.

A woman their age told me The Kizito Massacre is more than a case of striking students against defaulting colleagues. She told me it is more than a school affair. That the massacre is part of a general trend of violence against a kind. Violence against women, often ignored and often dismissed as normal.

If this terrible happening tells us anything and if it must be understood in its circumstances, you are free to think otherwise, then it must be a case of strong men fighting weak women. Far fetched as it may sound, it is part of a sexist sickness symptomatic of a chauvinistic culture.

The boy students-would-be- men were imposing their will on

innocuous women. But we need an experience so terrifying before we can condemn such violence? When this was taking place,
another woman was being threatened with rape in a Kiambu
school.

A parallel experience elsewhere will contextualise this men
sickness: In 1989, a lone enraged man wielding a gun invaded a
Montreal campus and massacred 14 women. He injured several
others. An individual can be psychotic, but how can we explain
collective madness such as was witnessed in a school?

Can we then understand these as violence against women so
endemic in paternalistic societies? In the Montreal case, tough
gun laws were imposed and anti-violence groups sprouted. It
was a tragedy so immeasurable. Yes, something was done.

Would closure of a school be a guarantee against a repeat of
such a massacre? Would making that school wholly girl or boy
school preempt such violence so unprovoked?

Something drastic better be done and that better be soon to
protect helpless women against brutal men.

Letter from the editor

by Hilary Ng'weno

Weekly Review, 19 July 1991, p. 1

The horror at St. Kizito Mixed Secondary School in Meru, where 19 girls died and dozens were raped following a rampage on girls' dormitories by boys, is a tragic statement about the breakdown of discipline in Kenya's schools, where violent demonstrations, strikes and riots leading to damage to property and injury to people have become common occurrences. But there is more to the St. Kizito incident than a mere breakdown in discipline in our schools. More graphically than any other event in recent years, this tragedy has underscored the abominable male chauvinism that dominates Kenyan social life. Despite what our laws say, and contrary to the high sounding rhetoric that spews out of pulpits and political platforms, the lot of our women and girls is lamentable. We treat them as second-class beings, good only for sexual gratification or burdensome chores. We bring up our boys to have little or no respect for girls. It is revealing, for instance, that those so adept at fulminating against the ills of society are generally silent about gender issues in this country. As we do a post mortem on the St. Kizito incident, we need to look into this deeper issue of the place and status of girls and women in our society. Women make up slightly more than half of our population. We are making enormous investments in their education at the primary school level. Economic commonsense ought to dictate that we treat our womenfolk with the respect that this investment entails. But there is more than economics at stake. There is basic human decency, and without inculcating in our male youth this human decency, we are going to have more St. Kizitos in the years to come.

Ministry should act promptly over children
by Mkanju
Sunday Nation, 21 July 1991, p. XII

Two weeks ago I observed that the Ministry of Education should do something about school children being left to fend for themselves in the dark while attending drama, music and other festivals.

I went as far as speculating that the Ministry would do nothing until tragedy called. I am sad to say that the St Kizito School tragedy illustrates this Kenyan habit.

Look at all the concern over the terribly inhuman act by the Kizito boys. Mr Sitima was there as were the politicians and local administration. This is as it should be. But do not wait until tragedy day.

Last year during the North Eastern Provincial Drama Festival I witnessed boys hurl stones at girls from North Eastern Province Girls School. A few years ago I also remember boys from the same province raiding the girls at night—stark naked: The event never hit the press. But Tom Sitima and his Provincial Education Officers (PEOs) know that boys molest girls in the schools; that the Ministry negligence has led to the suffering of many of our children. Nobody has lifted a finger because there was no Kizito.

There will be many a hasty solution offered now: separate girls from boys is going to reign supreme and the nation might embark on another costly exercise.

But maybe we should be asking ourselves what it is in schools that leads to Kizito. Are similar interpersonal relationships to be found in our homes? Perhaps there is need to tread with care. I saw the dignitaries on television, I saw the dishevelled death chamber dormitory and the doctor explaining the condition of a girl whom we all would have loved to hear speak. I hope this is not the route we will follow to get to the heart of the matter.

And Hon. Oloo Aringo and all the merry men from the Ministry: I am still asking what you have done or are doing to see to it that when the kids converge in Nairobi soon they will not be suffering yet again.

Family violence:
Women's bodies take up the cudgel
By Cecilia Kamau

Kenya Times, 1 August 1991, pp. 1, 2
[accompanied by photographs of Mrs. Mugo and Mrs. Onsando]

Women leaders have called on all Kenyans to root out, once and for all all causes of abuse against women and female children. A joint statement by Maendeleo ya Wanawake and the Kenya Business and Professional Women's Organisation called on the Government to set up "family courts" in all districts to put paid to the arousing gender-based domestic violence.

The statement said women's anger had been kindled by the recent St Kizito tragedy where 19 girls were killed and over 70 girls raped. The statement following a joint meeting of the premier women's organisations, declared that the St Kizito boys action had been legitimised by society's subordination of women and girls' importance.

The statement signed by the business and professional women's chairman Mrs Beth Mugo, and the chairman of Kanu Maendeleo, Mrs Wilkista Onsando, called women to vote wisely next time and elect to Parliament only leaders who are responsible and sensitive to women's and children's issues.

The full statement said: "We, the concerned women of Kenya, representing our individual selves and women's organisations, met on Monday to discuss the current wave of abuse and violence against women and girls, have observed and jointly decided:

• "That we wish to register our appreciation for the concern showed President Moi over the St Kizito School tragedy by his visit personally to the victims and the subsequent appointment of a committee of inquiry into the matter. We are prepared and willing to make our contribution to the inquiry.

• "That we condemn in the strongest terms the behaviour of the students and the administration of St Kizito and others who have been perpetrating the acts of violence against women and girls.

- "That rape is not just a crime. It is a *crime* that destroys one psychologically, emotionally and is a permanent mental injury on the victim.
- "That the St Kizito incident is just a mirror of the kind of abuse and violence that women and girls are going through in Kenya, at home, at the work place and in public places.

"It is not surprising, therefore, that for their action, the St Kizito boys found legitimacy from the way the Kenyan society subordinates women and girls.

- "That we strongly refute the assumption that abuse, rape and violence against women and girls is part of any culture in Kenya or elsewhere.
- "That we note with deep regret the way the St Kizito tragedy has sparked a wave of violence against girls all over the country.

"We propose the following action:

- "That women are now determined to stand against all forms of abuse and violence against them and their children.
- "We are calling on our society to start addressing the root cause of violence and abuse on women and children.
- "We are calling on the women of Kenya, as the majority of voters, to use their vote wisely to elect only leaders who are responsible and sensitive to women's and children's issues.
- "We call upon women's organisations and women as individuals to institute an educational programme to sensitise society on the gender issues and the status of women. The programme should provide support to victims of violence and abuse.
- "We call on the Government to set up family courts in all districts to deal with domestic violence against women and girls.
- "The Kenyan adult population, including parents, religious, political and other leaders, should re-examine or analyse themselves to see how they may have contributed to influencing the behaviour of Kenya's youth."

In an incident that shocked the world, 19 of the girls died at St Kizito Mixed Secondary School in Tigania, Meru, when the boss staged a midnight riot. Seventy-one of the girls were raped and scores injured.

Twenty-nine of the boys have been arraigned in court with 10 others still in custody, helping the police with investigations.

Some of the girls who were admitted to hospital have been discharged and all of them have been distributed to other schools. The school's headmaster, Mr James Laibuni, has been interdicted. Two hundred and sixty-five girls of the school have since been transferred to nine other schools in Meru District.

The education secretary of the Catholic Diocese of Meru, Father Francis Mbijjiwe, last week said that the church which sponsors the school, will change the name so that the boys are not haunted by it. The church with the help of Tigania people has promised to build a school for girls only in the area.

Rape: Why the apathy?

By Rasna Warah

Sunday Nation, 4 August 1991, p. viii

"I have never been free of the fear of rape. From a very early age, I, like most women, have thought of rape as part of my natural environment—something to be feared and prayed against like fire or lightning. I never asked why men raped; I simply thought it one of the many mysteries of human nature."

—Susan Griffin in an article entitled
"Rape: the All-American Crime" (1971).

The July 13 massacre in which 19 girls died and over 70 raped by their fellow students at Kizito Mixed Secondary School in Meru brings to mind two other mindless incidents of violence that shocked the world recently.

One is the 1983 case in New Bedford, Massachusetts in the US, of a woman who was raped repeatedly on a bar-room pool table for two hours while patrons of the bar cheered the rapists on. Even though two separate juries found four of the six defendants guilty of aggravated rape, most residents of the largely Portuguese-speaking American town were not asking themselves why they had allowed such a horrific incident to occur; rather, they were questioning the morality and character of the victim. Even ABC television's prime time show *Nightline* wondered what the woman was doing in the bar in the first place.

The other is the case in Montreal, Canada, which occurred one-and-a-half years ago when Marc Lepine —a failed engineering student—murdered 14 female engineering students on a Montreal campus. "I hate feminists," were among Lepine's last words before he committed suicide. In a letter he explained: "I have decided to send the feminists who almost ruined my life to their maker. They have always enraged me. They wanted to keep all the advantages of women and at the same time monopolise those of men."

For me, the New Bedford and Montreal incidents are not so dissimilar from the tragic case in Meru. All three are illustrations of a deep-seated contempt of women, exacerbated by unbelievable apathy on the part of society in preventing such crimes against women and legitimised through perpetuation of various rape myths such as "she asked for it" or "rapists are sexually starved psychopaths."

Rape is not about sexual gratification; it is about violence and humiliation. For example, a common practice in war is to kill the men and rape the women. Both killing and raping the enemy in the context of war have the same goal: the humiliation and subjugation of the victim. I therefore do not subscribe to the much touted theory that rape is a result of "indiscipline" because even the most disciplined armies in the world have committed this unforgivable crime. Rape is also used by insecure men to "teach women a lesson" or to "put them in their place." And that is exactly what the boys at Kizito did.

School attack inspires action by women of Kenya

by Michele Landsberg

Toronto Star, 12 October 1991, p. F1

The horror story from Kenya flashed around the world last July: boys at a government boarding school—angry because a soccer game had been cancelled—decided to vent their spite on the girls. They rampaged through a girls' dormitory, raping 71 of the female students. Nineteen girls died, some of them crushed beneath toppling iron bunk beds.

The story was vile enough in itself. My reaction shifted to appalled astonishment, however, when I read a comment by the school's vice-principal, Joyce Kithira: "The boys never meant any harm against the girls. They just wanted to rape."

A local probation officer told newspapers that rape at co-ed boarding schools was a common occurrence: "If you're a girl, you take it and hope you don't get pregnant."

Ripped out of all context, the story of St. Kizito boarding school was enough to revive hateful stereotypes of "the Dark Continent." The story troubled me all summer. I was sure there was more to learn. What, for example, did the women of Kenya have to say? Surely they didn't accept this brutality in passive silence? But, as with so many international stories, this one sizzled like sudden lightning across the front page and then vanished into oblivion.

Last week in Nairobi, I learned that the St. Kizito story has gone on reverberating in Kenyan society and—like our own Montreal massacre—has galvanized the women's movement to new energy. A massive coalition of women's groups met recently for the first time to present a strongly worded brief on women's equality to a presidential commission of inquiry into "unrest in the schools."

One small, hastily formed group in that coalition is called

Mothers in Action. In a bare-bones office of the Kenyan Child Welfare Association, I met with 10 of its members.

"When I heard the news the morning after, I was in shock, devastated," said Njoki Wainaina, echoing the feelings of many Canadians when we heard about the Ecole Polytechnique slaughter. "I couldn't bear feeling so helpless. I started to phone my friends."

Njoki, the co-ordinator of FEMNET (an African women's network), is a soft-spoken and compelling presence, long active in the Kenyan women's movement. Since the end of a U.N. women's conference in Nairobi in 1985, local feminists had busied themselves in individual efforts, setting up women's health services, for example, or working in development projects. Their public advocacy against sexual exploitation and violence was muted, partly in keeping with a more reserved style of public discussion of "unpleasant topics."

"By our silence, it had come to this," Njoki said mournfully. She and her friends grieved that the girls of St. Kizito had had so little encouragement to fight back. "We failed to tell them that they are not sexual objects."

The Mothers in Action include professors, doctors, journalists, graduate students and counsellors. Gathered around a long table for a rushed noon-hour meeting, the women told me about the letter they had written to the St. Kizito survivors, addressed to "Dear Daughter" and gently offering consolation and help.

"We wanted them to know that no matter what anyone says, rape is evil and totally unacceptable," said one member.

Just as we helped ourselves to a quick working lunch of samosas and lemon soda someone knocked at the door with the mail—including, dramatically, the first two responses from the girls of St. Kizito. (The girls, all between the ages of 14 and 18, are now scattered among different boarding schools. St. Kizito has closed and 32 boys are facing trial, variously charged with rape, attempted rape and manslaughter).

Excitedly, one member of the group volunteered to read the letters aloud to the rest of us.

Poignantly open responses

"'My dear mums," began the first, "We realize we are not alone . . . Our teachers are helping us but here at school I am lonely. I am mentally and physically disturbed and not concentrating well on my studies. . . .'"

"Thank you for remembering the girls who survived the tragedy," wrote the second youngster. "I was crushed under a bed for three hours . . . I wait for more encouragement from you."

All of us looked down at the table, hard, to hide our tears as we listened to the girls' poignantly open responses.

Yet I was exhilarated, too, to sense the determination, the indignation of Kenyan women that was suddenly bursting into the open in the wake of St. Kizito.

Already, the Mothers have published Nairobi's first anti-rape pamphlet "Women! Girls! You Can Defend Yourselves!" They are planning to open Peace House, a pioneering shelter for abused women. And work has begun on a commemorative quilt made up of patches to honor each of the 19 St. Kizito dead, and eventually to memorialize other victims of sexual violence.

The Mothers in Action buoyed my faith in the great worldwide movement to equality. Deep-rooted sexism—wherever it exists and however it's excused in the name of "traditional values"—leads inexorably to rape and violence. But everywhere, there are strong women who will rise against it.

Rape: Violation of woman's rights

by Esther Kamweru

Sunday Standard, 26 April 1992, pp. iv–v
*[accompanied by four frontal photographs of rape suspects
and one photograph of a victim with her face obscured]*

Nothing that a woman does or says gives a man the licence to her body unless she consents to it. I would hate to think that those men I know and admire would be so lacking in self-control that they would shed off their many positive attributes and rape a woman, however provocative her dress.

All indications in the recent months show that rape is a big issue. And rather than handle it as the serious societal problem that it is, as a violation of a woman's body and rights, the Catholic Archbishop of Nairobi chose to blame it on women, on the way they dress.

Said he: "By dressing up indecently, you (women) are inviting devilish deeds, rape included . . . Why dress up like this and then blame rape on men?"

Does provocative dressing provoke men into rape? Perhaps a look at who the Kenyan victims of rape are may help answer this question. A casual glance at back issues of newspapers shows that reported cases of rape involved minors and women who may have little, if any, thoughts of provocative dressing. The reports are shocking to say the least.

For example:

JANUARY 1992: Thirty-eight-year-old John Makanyanga Wandava pleaded guilty in court to defiling a three-year-old at Kaptatati Scheme in Uasin Gishu District. To make matters worse the child was found to be infected with a venereal disease. At three years old!

FEBRUARY 1992: John Mundio pleaded guilty in a Kisumu court of raping his two young sisters all night. The girls were nine and

13 years. Mundio said he was living alone since his wife had abandoned him hence his forced attentions on his own sisters!

FEBRUARY 1992: James Mwangi Chomba appeared in court for defiling (read rape) a six-year-old girl in Thigirichi Village in Kirinyaga District. According to evidence, Chomba had asked the little girl to accompany him to a nearby river where he raped her. Her genitals were seriously injured and she was even admitted to hospital for three months. Her mental and emotional health were not mentioned. The little girl's parents were away in church when the crime was committed.

MARCH 1992: Nineteen-year-old Njogi ole Maika admitted that he raped a married woman who he had found herding cows in desolate bushes in Kajiado District.

MARCH 1992: Ngonyo Mwagandi admitted raping his own daughter, a Std 5 pupil in Mwijo Village in Kilifi District.

MARCH 1992: A twelve-year-old girl was raped by a sixty-year-old man in Changamwe's Chaani Estate. The girl bled profusely for more than one hour after her genitals were ruptured. She was admitted to Coast General Hospital in critical condition.

MARCH 1992: A young Form 3 student walking with ber boyfriend in Central Park Nairobi was raped all night by two administration policemen. Pictures of her in newspapers showed a very soberly dressed young woman.

Experts have advanced several possible reasons that drive a man to rape and none of them touches on a woman's manner of dressing. Granted, this may arouse or even heighten desire but going as far as rape is I think too much. In fact, I consider the suggestion that a normal man can actually rape, whatever the provocation, an insult to all decent men.

According to experts, one group of potential rapists are men who have an inferiority complex. They have a need to feel powerful and strong, to assert their power over the physically weaker (it is assumed) woman. They have a desire to make women submit to their whims and thus prove their masculinity.

Another potential rapist according to experts is a man who is frustrated at work and who needs to show that he is in control somewhere. He too has feelings of inferiority.

Other experts say that woman is traditionally viewed as the property of many a man, to answer to his every call and administer to his every need. Many men who hold such views have no scruples about forceful sex especially of their wives.

Psychologists say that rapists are mentally sick people who belong to hospitals rather than prisons. They need counselling rather than prison sentences. In this category of rapists are those who abuse little girls and helpless house girls.

A rape victim goes through a traumatic experience. Children who are raped are bewildered and physically hurt.

It is said that this trauma follows them into adulthood where they have problems in sexual relationships. Many need intense therapy to snap out of it

The Archbishop's remarks are an example of what makes rape victims think that the crime was somehow their fault: A factor that makes them reluctant to talk about it, let alone report it to the police for legal redress.

The matter of blaming suggestive dressing for rape and making the victim feel guilty rather than aggrieved was extensively dealt with in the film, *The Accused*. Jodie Foster as the rape victim had been accused of provoking a gang of men into raping her. Her dress and her suggestive manner of dancing were the provocations cited. However, the jury of the film ruled that this was no justification for rape. Though only a film, I consider this a major contribution to the whole issue and how society sees the problem.

According to statistics released by the police in February this year, Rift Valley led in reported cases of rape in the whole country. 139 cases were reported in that province. Central Province came second with 126 reported cases. North Eastern had 7, Coast had 23, Nyanza 33, Western 36, Nairobi 70, Eastern 81.

Granted that rape is an issue that needs careful thought, and much more serious thought, what do leaders think about it and the sentences it carries? Some of them gave their views to the Law Reform Commission on the rights of the child last year. The commission visited various towns seeking people's opinions on various issues. Those who were given audience by the commission included lawyers, doctors, psychologists, social scientists and educationists.

High Court judge Lady Justice Effie Owuor regretted the amount of proof courts demanded in sexual offences, a trend that she felt favoured the culprits. She said suspects were known to go free or escape with light sentences even where evidence against them was overwhelming. "Ours is a sorry state when it comes to sexual offences, hence the high incidence of rape.'"

Giving his contribution, Mombasa DC, Mr John K. Nge'no said that courts should mete out stiffer sentences against child rapists since their deed left permanent scars on the victims.

"As it stands now, the sentences are too lenient on thc offenders."

And giving his views to the same commission in Nairobi during the same period, Nairobi Provincial Commissioner, Mr Fred Waiganjo, also called for stiffer penalties for those found guilty of defilement or rape in order to discourage them.

Many of those who gave their views stressed on the importance of a consolidated Act to protect the child in all circumstances.

Organisations such as the Business and Professional Women's Group and Mothers in Action have also been very vocal on the issue of rape. Mrs Joyce Umbima of Mothers in Action earlier in the year told an APS writer that "'Women are seen as tempters or evil . . . in the church circles. The issue of rape and violence against women has existed in society throughout the years. Now is the time to wake up and speak out against violence and degradation of women."

She is quoted as saying that men and women in churches must begin to openly speak out against rape and understand the psychological and emotional damage that a woman experiences in rape.

Another organisation that believes that there is an urgent need for society to appreciate the seriousness of the crime and try to curb its ocurrence is the Women Resource Centre of Kangemi. So seriously do they take the issue that they organised a two-day workshop and an open day in December last year to discuss it.

At the end of it all, the workshop gave 17 recommendations some of which were:

• In trial proceedings, the doctor's report should be sufficient evidence to convict upon and the victim's testimony should only reinforce this and be given when it is absolutely necessary.

• Organisations and individuals with resources and commitment should organise awareness raising activities in order to change people's attitude to rape victims.

• In marriage, the wife's consent to intercourse should not be presumed and a provision should be made in our laws to protect married women from matrimonial sexual abuse.

• More doctors should be attached to police stations and if possible women doctors should examine rape victims. Furthermore, doctors are encouraged to volunteer such services.

• Courts should administer stiffer penalties, on offenders to deter other would be rapists.

• To protect women from sexual abuse, cases of defilement should always be reported.

• Women should show solidarity by following rape cases and if need be to protest by way of demonstrations.

• Rape cases should be heard in camera.

The Kenya Anti-Rape organisation is today in the forefront in as regard rape issues. Reacting to the suggestion that women's way of dressing leads to their being raped, the organisation's secretary-general Ms Fatma Abeyd Anyanzwa said that it was actually lack of self-control on the part of the rapist that was responsible.

"It is natural that men and women get attracted to each other regardless of the way or manner of dress. But the most important issue is the sense of self control," she said. With all these people lobbying for stiffer sentences for rapists and for more protection for women and children in law, it is a wonder that nothing seems to have been done so far. Perhaps more church leaders, politicians and lawyers, doctors and others in society need to give it more thought and action.

Superficial and offguard remarks will not do. Neither will one sex blaming the other. This is a problem that should be given the seriousness it deserves.

Notes

References to the following publications will appear in abbreviated form: Agence France Presse (AFP); Associated Press (AP); *Daily Nation* (*DN*); *Kenya Times* (*KT*); *Standard* (*S*); *Sunday Nation* (*SN*); *Sunday Standard* (*SS*); *Sunday Times* (*ST*); *Weekly Review* (*WR*).

Preface

1. Although here and throughout the manuscript I use the singular word crime to refer to the murders and rapes at St. Kizito, I am aware that many crimes, in fact, occurred.

Chapter 1. Context of the St. Kizito Crime

1. Perry Anderson, "The Antinomies of Antonio Gramsci," *New Left Review* 100 (Nov. 1976–Jan. 1977): 5–78. See especially p. 21 for a discussion of the dialectic between force and consent, violence and civilization, and domination and hegemony in Gramsci's theory.

2. Louis Althusser, *Lenin and Philosophy and Other Essays*, translated by B. Brewster (London: New Left Books, 1971).

3. John Fiske, "British Cultural Studies and Television," in *Channels of Discourse, Reassembled*, ed. Robert C. Allen (Chapel Hill: Univ. of North Carolina Press, 1992), 287.

4. See Antonio Gramsci, *Selections from the Prison Notebooks*, edited and translated by Q. Hoare and G. Nowell-Smith (New York: International Publishers, 1971). I am additionally indebted to Chantal Mouffe's and Perry Anderson's interpretations of Gramsci,

specifically: Chantal Mouffe, "Hegemony and Ideology in Gramsci," in *Gramsci and Marxist Theory*, ed. Chantal Mouffe (London: Routledge & Kegan Paul, 1979), 168–204; Anderson, "The Antinomies."

5. Gramsci, 377.

6. Mouffe, 181.

7. Gramsci, 57.

8. Mouffe, 182–83.

9. Gramsci, 182.

10. Mouffe, 192.

11. For discussions of media values and constraints that affect news, see, for instance, Todd Gitlin, *The Whole World Is Watching: Mass Media and the Making and Unmaking of the New Left* (Berkeley: Univ. of California Press, 1980) and Gaye Tuchman, *Making News: A Study in the Construction of Reality* (New York: The Free Press, 1978). For a discussion of how news values and traditions apply to crime news see Steve Chibnall, *Law-and-Order News* (London: Tavistock, 1977).

12. Gitlin, *The Whole World*.

13. Althusser, *Lenin and Philosophy*. For a discussion of standard categories of liberal, radical, Marxist and socialist feminism, see Allison Jaggar, *Feminist Politics and Human Nature* (Sussex: The Harvester Press, 1983), 261. For applications of feminist theory, especially socialist feminism, to media studies, see, e.g., H. Leslie Steeves, "Feminist Theories and Media Studies," *Critical Studies in Mass Communication* 4:2 (1987): 95–135; H. Leslie Steeves and Rebecca A. Arbogast, "Feminism and Communication in Development: Ideology, Law, Ethics, Practice, " in B. Dervin and U. Hariharan, eds., *Progress in Communication Sciences*, vol. 11 (Norwood, N.J.: Ablex, 1993): 229–77; and H. Leslie Steeves, "Creating Imagined Communities: Development Communication and the Challenge of Feminism," *Journal of Communication* 43:3 (summer 1993): 218–29.

14. See Liesbet van Zoonen, *Feminist Media Studies* (London: Sage, 1994), for a discussion of feminist cultural studies and the influence of socialist feminism on these studies.

15. See especially Stuart Hall, "Encoding/Decoding," in *Culture, Media and Language: Working Papers in Cultural Studies, 1972–79*, ed. S. Hall, D. Hobson, A. Lowe, and P. Willis (London: Hutchinson, 1980), 128–38.

16. For overviews of scholarship around the world, see Margaret

Gallagher, *Unequal Opportunities: The Case of Women and the Media* (Paris: The UNESCO Press, 1981); Margaret Gallagher, "Women and Men in the Media," *Communication Research Trends* 12:1 (1992): 1–36; John Lent, *Women and Mass Communication: An International Annotated Bibliography* (Westport, Conn.: Greenwood Press, 1991); UNESCO, *Communication in the Service of Women: A Report on Action and Research Programmes, 1980–1985* (Paris: UNESCO, 1985); H. Leslie Steeves, "Gender and Mass Communication in a Global Context," in *Women in Mass Communication,* 2d ed., ed. Pamela Creedon (Newbury Park, Calif.: Sage, 1993), 32–60. For studies on representations of women in African media, see also: Esther Adagala and Wambui Kiai, "Folk, Interpersonal and Mass Media: The Experience of Women of Africa," in *Women Empowering Communication: A Resource Book on Women and Globalization of Media,* eds. Margaret Gallagher and Lilia Quindoza-Santiago. (New York: Women's International Tribune Centre, 1994), 11–35. An ongoing U.S. survey of newspapers and television newscasts is the Women, Men and Media project, which publishes an annual report. See, for instance, Women, Men and Media Project, *Slipping from the Scene: News Coverage of Females Drops* (Alexandria, Va.: Unabridged Communications, 1995).

17. Wagaki Mwangi, "Assessment of the Portrayal of Women in Kenyan Print Media, before, during and after the United Nations Decade for Women," unpublished research paper, School of Journalism, University of Nairobi, Nairobi, Kenya, 1991. Victoria N. Goro and Sophie A. Muluka-Lutta, "An Analysis of the Roles Portrayed by Women in Television Advertising: Nature and Extent of Sexism Present," unpublished research paper, School of Journalism, University of Nairobi, Nairobi, Kenya, 1991. Catherine Njeri Rugene, "The Portrayal of Women in the Humour Columns of the Sunday Newspapers," unpublished research paper, School of Journalism, University of Nairobi, Nairobi, Kenya, 1991. Anne Obura, *Changing Images: Portrayal of Girls and Women in Kenyan Textbooks* (Nairobi, Kenya: Acts Press, 1991).

18. Nancy Worthington, "Classifying Kenyan Women: Press Representations of Gender in Nairobi's 'Daily Nation,'" *Women's Studies in Communication* 18:1 (spring 1995): 65–84. Bonnie Dow, "Hegemony, Feminist Criticism and the Mary Tyler Moore Show," *Critical Studies in Mass Communication* 7 (1990): 261–74. Shuchiao E. Yang, "Critical Approaches to the Study of Women's Magazines: A

Review and Case Study of 'Singleness' in The Woman," (master's thesis, University of Oregon, 1993).

19. Clifford Krauss, "Confrontation in the Gulf; Baghdad Seals off the Exit of Foreigners across Border," *New York Times*, 10 Aug. 1990, sec. A, p. 1.

20. For a discussion of the prevalence of wartime rape, see, e.g., Catharine A. MacKinnon, "Turning Rape into Pornography: Postmodern Genocide," *Ms.* 4:1 (1993): 24–30.

21. Helen Benedict, *Virgin or Vamp: How the Press Covers Sex Crimes* (New York: Oxford Univ. Press, 1992). For examples of other studies revealing patriarchal bias in media accounts of gender violence, see: G. Finn, "Taking Gender into Account in the 'Theatre of Terror': Violence, Media and the Maintenance of Male Dominance," *Canadian Journal of Women and the Law* 3:2 (1989–1990): 375–94; Lisa M. Cuklanz, "News Coverage of Ethnic and Gender Issues in the Big Dan's Rape Case," in *Feminist Media Studies in a Global Setting: Beyond Binary Contradictions and into Multicultural Spectrums*, ed. Angharad N. Valdivia (Thousand Oaks, Calif.: Sage, 1995), 145–62; Marian Meyers, "News of Battering," *Journal of Communication* 44:2 (1994): 47–63.

22. Elizabeth Farstad, "News Coverage of the New Bedford Rape Case" (master's thesis, University of Oregon, 1989).

23. I am aware of one other study thus far on the press coverage of St. Kizito, by Susan Hirsch, "Interpreting Media Representations of a 'Night of Madness:' Law and Culture in the Construction of Rape Identities," *Law and Social Inquiry* 19(4) (fall 1994): 1023–1058. Though feminist in orientation, Hirsch's study differs from this one in its focus on comparing the Kenyan versus U.S. coverage, especially "legal constructions of rape identities" in each national context (p. 1023). Additionally, the research examines a limited Kenyan press sample from two publications: *The Daily/Sunday Nation* (six stories cited, all but one published in July 1991) and *The Weekly Review* (citations only from the July 19, 1991 issue). The U.S. sample also is small (six stories cited, all within a month of the crime). The study's documentation is therefore thin, and some observations are undocumented. Further, the study neglects the role of news values and traditions in the coverage, resulting in some disputable interpretations of differences between Kenyan and U.S. reports.

24. All quotes in this paragraph are from Jaggar, 261.

25. For a discussion of the Vienna Human Rights Conference, see Margaret Schuler's introduction to her *Claiming Our Place: Working the Human Rights System to Women's Advantage* (Washington, D.C.: Institute for Women, Law and Development, 1993), 4. UNIFEM's publications include: Roxanna Carrillo, *Battered Dreams: Violence against Women as an Obstacle to Development* (New York: UNIFEM, 1992); and Lori Heise, *Fact Sheet on Gender Violence: A Statistics for Action Facts Sheet* (New York: IWTC/UNIFEM Resource Centre, 1992).

26. Information on the United Nations Fourth World Conference on Women held in Beijing may be found on the Internet at http://www.igc.apc.org/womensnet/beijing/un/un.html. Another web site containing conference documents, document summaries and related information is: http://www.iisd.ca/linkages/4wcw/backinfo.html. See also United Nations, *The United Nations and the Advancement of Women, 1945–1996.* (New York: United Nations, 1996) This publication (The United Nations Blue Books Series, Volume VI, revised edition) contains more than 130 U.N. documents related to women's rights, including the outcome of the 1995 Fourth World Conference on Women.

27. For examples of antigender violence activism in local contexts, see for instance, Margaret Schuler, ed., *Freedom from Violence: Women's Strategies from around the World* (New York: UNIFEM, 1992).

28. E.g., Farstad.

29. Peggy Reeves Sanday, "Silencing the Feminine," in *Rape: An Historical and Social Enquiry*, ed. Silvana Tomaselli and Roy Porter (New York: Basil Blackwell, 1986), 95; David Levinson, *Family Violence in Cross-Cultural Perspective* (Newbury Park, Calif.: Sage, 1989); Lori L. Heise, "Gender-Based Abuse: The Global Epidemic," in *Reframing Women's Health: Multidisciplinary Research and Practice*, ed. Alice J. Dan (Thousand Oaks, Calif.: Sage, 1994), 233–50. I am grateful to Carolyn Stewart Dyer for calling my attention to Peggy Reeves Sanday and many of the other sources used in this section.

30. For elaboration and evidence on the points made in this paragraph, see Susan Brownmiller's classic work: *Against Our Will: Men, Women, and Rape* (New York: Simon & Schuster, 1975). See also: Susan Estrich, *Real Rape* (Cambridge, Mass.: Harvard Univ. Press, 1987); Nancy Gager and Cathleen Schurr, *Sexual Assault: Confronting Rape in America* (New York: Grosset & Dunlap, 1976); Gilbert Geis,

"Group Sexual Assaults," *Medical Aspects of Human Sexuality* 5:5 (1971): 100–113; Margaret T. Gordon and Stephanie Riger, *The Female Fear* (New York: Free Press, 1989); A. Nicholas Growth with H. Jean Birnbaum, *Men Who Rape: The Psychology of the Offender* (New York: Plenum Press, 1979); Patricia A. Rozee-Koker and Glenda C. Polk, "The Social Psychology of Group Rape," *Sexual Coercion & Assault* 1:2 (1986): 57–65; Peggy Reeves Sanday, *Fraternity Gang Rape: Sex, Brotherhood, and Privilege on Campus* (New York: New York Univ. Press, 1990); Silvana Tomaselli and Roy Porter, eds., *Rape: An Historical and Social Enquiry* (New York: Basil Blackwell, 1986).

31. Gager and Schurr, 220.

32. The phrase quoted is from Rozee-Koker and Polk, "Group Rape," 58. See also: Geis, "Group Sexual Assaults"; Sanday, *Fraternity Gang Rape*; Julie K. Ehrhart and Bernice R. Sandler, *Campus Gang Rape: Party Games?* (Washington, D.C.: Project on the Status and Education of Women, 1985).

33. The quote is from Rozee-Koker and Polk, 58. See also Geis, "Group Sexual Assaults"; Sanday, "Silencing the Feminine"; Sanday, *Fraternity Gang Rape*.

34. Rozee-Koker and Polk, 64.

35. Sanday, "Silencing the Feminine"; Levinson, *Family Violence.*

36. For data on women's involvement in farm labor, see George M. Ruigu, *Women Employment in Kenya* (Nairobi, Kenya: Univ. of Nairobi, Institute for Development Studies, 1985), 13–14. See also Republic of Kenya, *Development Plan 1994–1996* (Nairobi: Government Printer, 1994), 254. For an overview of rural women's disadvantages in the areas listed see, e.g., Maria Nzomo and Kathleen Staudt, "Man-Made Political Machinery in Kenya: Political Space for Women?" in *Women and Politics Worldwide*, ed. Najma Chowdhury and Barbara Nelson (New Haven, Conn.: Yale Univ. Press, 1994), 416–35. See also Kathleen Staudt, *Agricultural Policy Implementation: A Case Study from Western Kenya* (West Hartford, Conn.: Kumarian Press, 1985).

37. Statistics correlating women's education and social change are indicated in World Bank, *World Development Report 1991: The Challenge of Development* (New York: Oxford Univ. Press, 1991), 55. See also, United Nations, *The World's Women 1995: Trends and Statistics* (New York: United Nations, 1995), chapter 4. Kenya Ministry of

Education statistics for 1989 indicate that females make up 41.4 percent of the students in Form I of secondary school, but that by Form VI, the percentage dropped to 32.2 percent. See Republic of Kenya, Central Bureau of Statistics, *Statistical Abstract, 1990* (Nairobi, Kenya: Government Printer, 1990), 187. For a discussion of sexual harassment and discrimination in schools, see "Sexism in Kenya: The Woman's Lot Is Not a Happy One," *WR*, 9 Aug. 1991, pp. 15–18. In a discussion of gender inequities in various employment categories, Ruigu, in *Women Employment* (19–20), notes that the "modern" sector employment in urban areas provides the highest wages and the best benefits, yet there is only about one woman for every five men in this sector of employment. This statistic is about the same for both public and private organizations (ibid., 28). Most of the few women present are in secretarial positions or in lower status manufacturing industries. In the informal sector (including sales in the open market), women constitute about 31.8 percent of employees. Women's near-absence in government policy-making roles is discussed in "Strategies to Bolster Women," *WR*, 28 Feb. 1992; Amnesty International, *Women in Kenya: Repression and Resistance* (London: Amnesty International, 1995). Amnesty International (2) notes that in July 1995 there were only six women members of Parliament, and Kenya's first woman cabinet minister was appointed in May, 1995. Nzomo and Staudt, in "Man-Made Political Machinery," cite data from throughout Africa to show that men's control of political machinery is even greater in Kenya than in many other African countries. In rural areas, they argue that while women have gained some grassroots power, this is inadequately translated into broader representation or equitable and appropriate consideration in development projects.

38. For discussions of variables contributing to women's oppression in post-colonial Kenya, see, for instance, Ester Boserup, *Women's Role in Economic Development* (New York: St. Martin's Press, 1970); and Nzomo and Staudt, "Man-Made Political Machinery." For a discussion of women in relation to communication and information organizations and policy in Kenya, see H. Leslie Steeves, "Women, Rural Information Delivery, and Development in Sub-Saharan Africa" (Michigan State University, Working Paper no. 212, 1990). Also, H. Leslie Steeves, "Sharing Information in Kenya: Communication and Information Policy Considerations and Conse-

quences for Rural Women," *Gazette* 52 (1996): 157–81. Also recommended is Center for Women's Global Leadership, *Gender Violence and Women's Human Rights in Africa* (New Brunswick, N.J.: Center for Women's Global Leadership, Douglass College, 1994).

39. Patricia Stamp, "Burying Otieno: The Politics of Gender and Ethnicity in Kenya," *Signs* 16:4 (1992): 808–45. Stamp borrows the term "collaborative hegemony" from Zakia Pathak and Rajeswari Sunder Rajan, "Shahbano," *Signs* 14:3 (1989): 569. I thank Kathleen Staudt for bringing Patricia Stamp's excellent article to my attention.

40. Stamp, 844.

41. Prominent women's organizations include the Maendeleo ya Wanawake Organization (MYWO), the National Council of Women of Kenya, the Women's Bureau of the Ministry of Culture and Social Services, the Kenya Business and Professional Women's Organization (KBPWO), the Kenya branch of AAWORD (African Association for Women's Research and Development), and the African Women Development and Communication Network (Femnet), which is headquartered in Nairobi. For a discussion of these organizations and their role in policy-making, see Nzomo and Staudt, "Man-Made Political Machinery." One critic of women's complacency is Kenyan political scientist and activist Dr. Maria Nzomo, who is quoted in "Taking the Bull by the Horns," *WR*, 13 Sept. 1991, pp. 15–18. Also, Dr. Nzomo was commissioned to write a paper on behalf of the Kenya branch of the Association of African Women for Research and Development (AAWORD), entitled "Women in Politics and Public Decision-Making." She presented the paper on 31 August, and was given prominence in "Women's Leaders Too Weak, Says Lecturer," *ST*, 1 Sept. 1991, pp. 1–2; and "Topple Men's Regime—Don," *KT*, 3 Sept. 1991, pp. 1–2. The paper also was published in full in the *KT* and *ST* in three parts: "Women as Men's Voting Tools," *KT*, 4 Sept. 1991, pp. 14–15; "Women Need to Unite with a Common Vision," *KT*, 6 Sept. 1991, pp. 20–21; and "Women's Passivity to Blame for Their Woes," *ST*, 8 Sept. 1991, pp. 12, 29. In the final *ST* story Nzomo refers to the St. Kizito aftermath as "the only time in recent years that women leaders have publicly come forward and taken a position on a national issue with gender dimensions" (29). Although Nzomo does note the weakness of women leaders and women's organizations, her analysis is sophisticated and does not merely blame

women, as two of the four headlines accompanying the *KT* stories imply.

42. A 1985 study by the Public Law Institute and the Women's Bureau in the Ministry of Culture and Social Services examines why victims and witnesses of gender violence don't speak out. See "Sexism in Kenya," *WR*, 9 Aug. 1991, p. 5. For a discussion of rape by security personnel, see Amnesty International, 12–13. See also a report in *Women's International Network News*, "Rape and Violence against Women in Kenya," 19:2, (spring 1993): 55.

43. Laws of Kenya, Chapter 63, *The Penal Code*, rev. ed. (Nairobi: Government Printer, 1985), Section 139. The law also is quoted and discussed in "Sexism in Kenya," *WR*, p. 13. In comparison, the FBI criminal code in the U.S. and also U.S. common law define rape as "carnal knowledge of a female forcibly and against her will" (quoted in Gordon and Riger, 57). One flaw in the Kenyan law is the implication that rape within marriage is acceptable, unless the assailant impersonates the victim's husband.

44. See Laws of Kenya, Chapter 63, Sections 140 and 145. See also "Sexism in Kenya," *WR*, p. 13.

45. "Sexism in Kenya" *WR*, p. 14.

Chapter 2. *Interpreting Press Accounts*

1. See Van Zoonen, 134–35. I use the label "qualitative content analysis" cautiously, as I realize this carries different meanings for different scholars. Peter K. Manning and Betsy Cullum-Swan, "Narrative, Content, and Semiotic Analysis," in *Handbook of Qualitative Research*, ed. Norman K. Denzin and Yvonna S. Lincoln (Thousand Oaks, Calif.: Sage, 1994), 463–77, divide the analysis of documentary data into the following categories: content and narrative analysis, structuralism and semiotics. According to their system, my application of Gitlin's framing approach is a "macrotextual narrative analysis." Other sources that make the points in this paragraph include: John Pauley, "A Beginner's Guide to Doing Qualitative Research," *Journalism Monographs* 125 (Feb. 1991); Robert K. Yin, *Case Study Research: Design and Methods* (Beverly Hills: Sage, 1984); Catherine Marshall and Gretchen B. Rossman, *Designing Qualitative Research* (Newbury Park: Sage, 1989); Catherine Kohler Reissman, *Narrative*

Analysis (Newbury Park: Sage, 1993); and Gitlin, *The Whole World*. See also many chapters, including the editors' Introduction, in Denzin and Lincoln, *Handbook*.

2. For a discussion of sampling in qualitative research see, e.g., Pauley, "A Beginner's Guide," 12. I was in Kenya for the first six weeks of this time period, when the bulk of the reporting took place, and hence saved all the local stories that appeared. Stories from the remainder of the year were obtained via a combination of interlibrary loan and the assistance of personnel at Northwestern University. Stories about St. Kizito were defined as stories that mentioned the incident. Some of these stories did not focus exclusively on St. Kizito, but were primarily about something directly related, e.g., newly formed anti-rape organizations. International stories were those that appeared in the omnifile of the database NEXIS (News Exchange Information System) after inserting the keywords "rape," "Kenya," "Meru," and "St. Kizito." This database was checked twice for stories that appeared the year following the crime: in summer 1993 and again in spring 1996. The NEXIS database is somewhat fluid and stories had been added in 1996 that did not appear in 1993. Likewise, a few stories that appeared in 1993 did not appear in 1996. From this database, I believe that I have obtained all international press accounts that use primary sources, and also that the stories obtained provide a good sampling of the range of accounts that appeared in global media. Obviously, this sample is neither comprehensive nor statistically random, however.

3. According to Adewale Maja-Pearce, "The Press in East Africa," *Index on Censorship* 21:7 (July/Aug. 1992): 60, "The *Daily Nation* is published by the Nation Group of Newspapers, owned by Prince Sadruddin Aga Khan. The company went public in 1989, when it sold off 60% of its shares. The identities of the shareholders have never been revealed." Whether this means that Kenyans partly own the *DN* is unknown and likely irrelevant as the Aga Kahn remains in control of the paper and necessary for its survival. According to a United Nations source, the circulation figures for the three Nairobi dailies are as follows: 160,000 *(DN)*, 54,000 *(S)*, and 30,000 *(KT)*. *DN* and *KT* additionally have Kiswahili editions, *Taifa Leo* and *Kenya Leo*, respectively. (*World Media Handbook: Selected Country Profiles, 1995 Edition*. New York: U.N. Department of Public Information, 1995 [(DP1/ 1614. Sales No. E.95.1.34), 156–57.])

In 1995 the ninety-three-year-old *Standard*, owned by Lonrho for twenty-seven years, was bought by close associates of President Moi, including his son, leaving Kenya with the *Nation* as its only privately owned newspaper. (See Charles Wachira, "Kenya-Media: President's Men Acquire Region's Oldest Paper," Inter Press Service, 29 Aug. 1995.) The Kenya African National Union, which owns the *Kenya Times*, is the party of President Moi and was the only party allowed by law between 1982 and 1991. Television is controlled almost entirely by KANU, and most viewers live in urban areas. In 1991 there were two television stations, and a third was launched in 1995. The Kenya Broadcasting Corporation (KBC), a parastatal, plays a major role in operating television in Kenya. KBC also broadcasts radio nationally in English and Kiswahili and regionally in up to sixteen local languages. (A parastatal is a relatively autonomous business that remains affiliated with government.)

4. Stuart Hall, Introduction to *Paper Voices: The Popular Press and Social Change, 1935–1965*, ed. A. C. H. Smith (London: Chatto & Windus, 1975), 15.

5. Specifically, Erving Goffman, *Frame Analysis: An Essay on the Organization of Experience* (New York: Harper and Row, 1974), describes how individuals frame reality in order to manage it. Gaye Tuchman applies Goffman's idea to media accounts of reality in *Making News* and in an earlier article, "Telling Stories," *Journal of Communication* 26:4 (Aug. 1976): 93–96.

6. Gitlin, *The Whole World*, 7. For a critical discussion of the framing concept, see Robert M. Entman, "Framing: Toward Clarification of a Fractured Paradigm," *Journal of Communication* 43:4 (autumn 1993): 51–58. Entman's definition (52) is similar to that of Todd Gitlin: "Framing essentially involves *selection* and *salience*. To frame is to *select some aspects of a perceived reality and make them more salient in a communicating text, in such a way as to promote a particular problem definition, causal interpretation, moral evaluation, and/or treatment recommendation* for the item described" (emphasis in original). As an example, Entman notes the "cold war" frame that was evident in U.S. international news for many years.

7. Gitlin, *The Whole World*, 27–28.

8. See Benedict, *Virgin or Vamp*, and Farstad, "New Bedford Rape Case." Farstad uses both quantitative and qualitative methods. She models her methods after the Glasglow Media Group, in which conceptual categories (in Farstad's case, patriarchal, socialist feminist, and liberal feminist perspectives) serve as a guide for identification

and interpretation. Glasgow Media Group, *More Bad News* (London: Routledge & Kegan Paul, 1980).

9. Length became more difficult to measure and compare after the first six weeks, as I obtained the stories via a combination of methods involving photocopies of varied reduction/enlargement made from both original news copy and microfilm.

10. For a discussion of the *etic* versus *emic* problem, see, e.g., Arthur J. Vidich and Stanford M. Lyman, "Qualitative Methods: Their History in Sociology and Anthropology," in *Handbook*, ed. N. K. Denzin and Y. S. Lincoln (Thousand Oaks, Calif.: Sage, 1994), 26. For a discussion of the export of Western news traditions to Africa, see, for instance, William A. Hachten, *The Growth of Media in the Third World: African Failures, Asian Successes* (Ames, Ia.: Iowa State Univ. Press, 1993). See also John Baptist Abuoga and Absalom Aggrey Mutere, *The History of the Press in Kenya* (Nairobi: African Council on Communication Education, 1988).

11. Van Zoonen, *Feminist Media Studies*, 146. See also Reissman, *Narrative Analysis*.

12. The Nyambenes are the focus of Paul Goldsmith's dissertation: "Symbiosis and Transformation in Kenya's Meru District" (doctoral dissertation, University of Florida, 1994). The quote is from p. 4. See also p. 48. For additional contextual information about the Nyambenes, see Gideon S. Were and Simiyu Wandibba, eds., *Meru District Socio-Cultural Profile* (Nairobi, Kenya: Government of Kenya and University of Nairobi, Classic Printers & Stationers Ltd., 1988). For maps of Kenya, see, e.g., Republic of Kenya, *Development Plan, 1994–1996*.

13. Goldsmith, "Symbiosis and Transformation," 90–94.

14. Goldsmith, "Symbiosis and Transformation," 63. Goldsmith's description is adapted from Jeffrey Fadiman, *Oral Traditions of the Meru of the Mt. Kenya Region* (Athens: Ohio Univ. Press, 1982).

15. See A. Kimokoti, "Education and Social Training." In *Meru District Socio-Cultural Profile*, eds. Gidion S. Were and Simiyu Wandibba (Nairobi, Kenya: Government of Kenya and University of Nairobi, Classic Printers & Stationers Ltd., 1988), 131.

16. In recent years there has been a tendency to have boys circumcised much younger, either at the hospital or at home. See A. Darkwa. "Music and Dance Traditions." In *Meru District Socio-Cultural Profile*, eds. Gidion S. Were and Simiyu Wandibba (Nairobi,

Kenya: Government of Kenya and University of Nairobi, Classic Printers & Stationers Ltd., 1988), 182.

17. Kimokoti, "Education and Social Training," 131. See also Akong'a, "Social Stratification," in *Meru District Socio-Cultural Profile*, eds. Gidion S. Were and Simiyu Wandibba (Nairobi, Kenya: Government of Kenya and University of Nairobi (Classic Printers & Stationers Ltd. 1988), especially 96–100.

18. H. Kalule, "Marriage and Related Customs," in *Meru District Socio-Cultural Profile*, eds. Gidion S. Were and Simiyu Wandibba (Nairobi, Kenya: Government of Kenya and University of Nairobi, Classic Printers & Stationers Ltd., 1988), especially p. 121–24. See also Akong'a, "Social Stratification."

19. In general, girls and women were expected to keep company with peers and avoid walking alone, or risk the accusation or reputation of prostitution. See, e.g., Akong'a, "Social Stratification."

20. Goldsmith, "Symbiosis and Transformation," 7.

21. Ibid.

22. Most frequent spelling in media accounts. Other spellings in stories: Laibon, Laibun, and Laibuni.

23. Initial reports state that the dead girls were not raped. Later, at the trials of accused boys, medical evidence was introduced that at least some of these girls also suffered rape or attempted rape.

24. The number of boys placed on probation varies in local and international accounts. A *DN* backpage story of 21 October 1992 (p. 20) headlined "St. Kizito Boys 'Successfully Rehabilitated,'" quotes Mr. Macharia Appolos, a criminologist and Meru District probation officer, announcing that all the boys placed on probation had been rehabilitated, that they were "comfortably settled in their new schools," and that his department was providing many of the boys with help to deal with "the psychological trauma of the tragedy."

25. Ngugi wa Mbugua, "St. Kizito: A Kenyan Nightmare that Won't Go Away," *SN*, 21 June 1992, Lifestyle Section, pp. 8–9. The girls' poor academic performance and inadequate counseling were also reported by James Schofield, "Kenya: New Name But Old Values Still Haunt Kenya's School of Infamy," *The Age* (Melbourne), 13 July 1992, Reuters, NEXIS.

26. Local stories noting rape as a factor in school strikes elsewhere and at St. Kizito before the 13–14 July crime include: Alex Riithi, "19 Girls Killed in School Rape," *KT*, 15 July 1991, pp. 1, 2;

Mwicigi Njoroge, "Seeking the Roots of Students' Indiscipline," *KT*, 20 July 1991, p. 18; Mugambi Karanja, "Kizito: Are We Qualified to Talk of Indiscipline?" *ST*, 21 July 1991, pp. 6–7; Alex Riithi, "Another St. Kizito Shocker, Questions that Weren't Answered," *KT*, 24 July 1991, pp. 1, 7; Schamallah Momo, "Who Were Behind the St. Kizito Tragedy," *ST*, 28 July 1991, p. 7; Kaburi Franz, Margaret Njoroge, and S. Wafala, "Stop Other Kizito Tragedies," *KT*, 29 July 1991, p. 7; Alex Riithi, "Kizito Phobia Sweeps Schools," *KT*, 31 July 1991, p. 3; Cecilia Kamau, "Family Violence: Women's Bodies Take up the Cudgel," *KT*, 1 Aug. 1991, pp. 1, 2; Willis Tsuma Musungu, "St. Kizito: We Should Encourage Counseling, Discipline in Schools," *KT*, 16 Aug. 1991, p. 7; Mkanjo, "Ministry Should Act Promptly over Children," *SN*, 21 July 1991, p. xii; Agnes Karanja, "St. Kizito is Society Problem," *DN*, 22 July 1991, p. 7; "Strokes for Boys Who Scared Girls," *DN*, 2 Aug. 1991, p. 1; "Kakamega Kizito Head Summoned," *DN*, 3 Aug. 1991, p. 3; Peter Angwenyi, "Parents Appeal for Girl Students' Security," *SN*, 4 Aug. 1991, p. 5; Raphael Kahaso, "Tragedy that Shocked All," *S*, 18 July 1991, p. 21; Enock Anjili, "Don't Exploit Women—Nuns," *S*, 22 July 1991, p. 14; Kihu Irimu, "Women in Plea over Violence," *S*, 1 Aug. 1991, p. 4; Patrick Wakhisi, "Six Picked up at Another St. Kizito," *S*, 2 Aug. 1991, p. 4; "Cane for Eighteen Bullies," *S*, 2 Aug. 1991, p. 5; Kidji Nduku, "Kenyan Women Are Angry," *S*, 7 Aug. 1991, pp. 17, 20.

27. Benedict, 8–9. For a general discussion of the connection between social prominence and amount of news coverage, see also Herbert Gans, *Deciding What's News: A Study of CBS Evening News, NBC Nightly News, Newsweek, and Time* (New York: Vintage Books, 1980).

28. The other front-page story in the *KT* was an editorial comparing St. Kizito to colonial barbarism. Philip Ochieng, "Dreadful Human Rights Violations," *KT*, 11 Sept. 1991, pp. 1, 6, 12. The other front-page story in the *DN* announced a memorial service marking the year anniversary of the crime. "St. Kizito Tragedy Memorial Service," *DN*, 13 July 1992, p. 1.

29. The two accused wardens were ultimately acquitted. Odhiambo-Orlale, "Not Guilty! Wardens in Julie Ward Trial Freed," *DN*, 30 June 1992, pp. 1–2.

30. Perhaps also both the Julie Ward and Mike Tyson trials provided a convenient means of avoiding the pain and national guilt evoked by St. Kizito.

31. My measurements have been adjusted for column width. Subtotals of column inches for the first seven days of media coverage (15–21 July) indicate less disparity between the three papers. The *Kenya Times* allocated 453 column inches, the *Daily Nation* 395 column inches, and *The Standard* 300 column inches.

32. Personal communication with Absalom Mutere, director of the School of Journalism, University of Nairobi, 29 Sept. 1993. Also, personal communication with a *Kenya Times* reporter, 1 Apr. 1994. According to the *KT* reporter, Ochieng could be a "tyrant" when he wanted stories quickly. Ochieng was fired in early October 1991. A *Weekly Review* story, "Ochieng Out in the Cold," 10 Oct. 1991, pp. 12–13, discusses his "quirky and controversial style."

33. Philip Ochieng, *I Accuse the Press: An Insider's View of the Media and Politics in Africa* (Nairobi: Initiatives Publishers, 1992), 136.

34. Benedict, 5.

35. Personal communication with Absalom Mutere, director of the School of Journalism, University of Nairobi, 29 Sept. 1993. According to Mutere, virtually all of the managerial staff, including assignment editors, are male and were at the time, except for one female managing editor at *The Standard*, Esther Kamweru. In addition, most reporters are male. Most females working at the papers are in sub-editor roles, meaning they edit stories for grammar, length, and spelling and write headlines. However, women are seldom in the majority in these roles and they do not have final say as to what the stories look like.

36. For sources of scholarship on this question, see Van Zoonen, especially chapter 4.

37. For anecdotal examples in the U.S. context, see Kay Mills, *A Place in the News* (New York: Dodd, Mead, 1988).

38. The first St. Kizito-related news story by a woman did not appear until 1 August: Kamau, "Family Violence," *KT*.

39. E.g., Gitlin, 80–81.

Chapter 3. Patriarchal Framing

1. Irungu Ndirangu, Imanene Imathiu, and KNA, "Moi Orders Thorough Investigation as . . . Rampaging Boys Leave 19 Girls Dead," *DN*, 15 July 1991, 1, 2.

2. Alex Riithi, "19 Girls Killed," *KT*, 15 July 1991, pp. 1–2.

3. Xavier Lugaga and Victor Nzomo, "Rampaging Students Flee After Incident . . . 19 girls Killed in Rape Ordeal," *S*,15 July 1991, p. 1.

4. "19 School Girls Die after Rape Ordeal," AFP, 14 July 1991, NEXIS; "Nineteen Kenyan Schoolgirls Killed in Dormitory Attack," Reuters, 14 July 1991, NEXIS; "Boys Raid Girls' Dorm; Many Raped, 19 Die," *The Washington Times*, 15 July 1991, p. A2, NEXIS; "Croatian Militia Retakes Four Serbian-Held Villages," *USA Today*, 15 July 1991, p. 4A, NEXIS; "Kurdish Leader Says Agreement is Near," *St. Petersburg Times*, 15 July 1991, p. 6A, NEXIS; Manoah Esipisu, "Kenyan School Closed after 19 Girls Die in Dormitory Raid," Reuters, 15 July 1991, NEXIS; "Nineteen Kenyan Girls Killed in Dorm Attack," *Orlando Sentinel Tribune*, 15 July 1991, p. A5, NEXIS; "19 Kenyan Girls Die in Teen Dorm Attack," *Chicago Tribune*, sec. News, p. 10, 15 July 1991, NEXIS; "19 School Girls Killed," *Newsday*, 15 July 1991, sec. News, p. 14, NEXIS; "Boys at Kenya School Rape Girls, Killing 19," *New York Times*, 15 July 1991 sec. A, p. 3, NEXIS.

5. "Meru Tragedy: Boys' Parents Get Ultimatum," *DN*, 16 July 1991, pp. 1–2. "Rampaging Boys Hide in Bush," *S*, 16 July 1991, p. 1; Ngumo was Kuria, "Moi to Visit Schools," *S*, 16 July 1991, p. 1; Murigi Macharia, "Meru Villagers Mourn Their Dead," *KT*, 16 July 1991, pp. 1–2. "The Victims," *S*, 16 July 1991, p. 1.

6. "Meru Tragedy," *DN*, pp. 1–2; "Rampaging Boys," *S*, p. 1, 13; Kuria, "Moi to Visit Schools," *S*, p. 1; Macharia, "Meru Villages," *KT*, pp. 1–2; "The Victims," *S*, p. 1.

7. "Why This Beastly Student Behavior?" *S*, 16 July 1991, p. 8; "Morals Were Never So Low in Schools," *DN*, 16 July 1991, p. 6.

8. Murigi Macharia, Alex Riithi, and KNA, "After Meru Co-education Tragedy . . . Moi Moves to Protect Girls," *KT*, 17 July 1991, p. 1, 18; *Standard* reporter and KNA, "Moi Sees 'Death Chamber' Horrors," *S*, 17 July 1991, pp. 1, 13; Irungu Ndirangu, "Death Dormitory Moves Moi to Tears," *DN*, 17 July 1991, p. 1, 18.

9. Imanene Imathiu, "71 Girls Raped in St. Kizito Tragedy," *DN*, 17 July 1991, pp. 1, 18; Victor Nzuma, Joseph Olweny, and Imanene Imathiu, "Leaders Condemn Girls' Killing," *DN*, 17 July 1991, p. 2.

10. Aringo quoted in Wamahiu Muya, "Team Named to Probe Indiscipline in Schools," *DN*, 18 July 1991, p. 1. See also *Times* reporter and KNA, "Kizito Rape Probe Opens . . . Team to Report to Moi in 3 Months," *KT*, 18 July 1991, pp. 1, 2. The report of the eleven-member indiscipline committee never received much public-

ity, and may not have been released to the public. The only story I found that mentioned it was in the *WR*, which noted that the committee "recommended that the number of subjects in the 8-4-4 system of education be reduced to ease the load on students, and that the sponsors of various schools exercise greater controls on their schools." "A Year Later: Taking Stock," *WR*, 17 July 1992, pp. 23–24. According to a later Inter Press Service report by Horace Awori, "Kenya: Castrate, Hang, Flog Rapists, Women Say," 18 March 1993, NEXIS, a written report was never released by this committee.

11. The only exception is the Inter Press Service's first story on the event. This feature story fails to even mention rape, but rather quotes labor minister Philip Masinde, who blames advocates of pluralism (including "disgruntled clergymen with foreign links") for inciting school riots. Horace Awori, "Kenya: Student Riots Shake up Nation," Inter Press Service, 17 July 1991, NEXIS.

12. Mwicigi Njoroge, "Aringo: Plotters Responsible for Children's Riots," *KT*, 18 July 1991, pp. 1,2. Francis Muroki, Amos Marenya, and John Kiama, "St. Kizito Boys Were Not Alone, Claims MP," *S*, 18 July 1991, p. 2. The only international story I found that repeated Peter Oloo Aringo's claim of foreign agitators is "Kenyan Riot Boys in Court," *The Times* (London), 30 July 1991, NEXIS. The only international stories that appear to use St. Kizito to promote a multiparty democracy are David Chazen, "Kenya's Social Tensions Highlighted by Schoolgirl Killings," AFP, 16 July 1991, NEXIS, which quotes Gitobu Imanyara, former editor of the *Nairobi Law Monthly* and courageous advocate for press freedom; and Robert M. Press, "Behind Kenya's Push for Multiparty Reform," *Christian Science Monitor*, 14 Aug. 1991, sec. The World, p. 4. Particularly blatant examples of efforts to blame church leaders or opposition politicians are two editorials in the *Kenya Times* by Philip Ochieng, the editor-in-chief at the time. In the first, "St. Kizito and the Pharisees in the Christian Church," *KT*, 22 July 1991, pp. 1, 6–7, Ochieng uses the fact that St. Kizito is a Catholic school to challenge the Catholic church (and all churches) to clean the skeletons out of their own closets before criticizing government. In the second, "Dreadful Human Rights Violation," *KT*, 11 Sept. 1991, pp. 1, 6, 12, Ochieng uses the incident to castigate human rights activists who criticize the government while remaining silent about the abuse of women, and who may even go home and beat their own wives.

13. Poor management, misuse of school finances, and poor dia-

logue between administrators and students were the primary assumed causes of indiscipline from the government's perspective. As I will note later, other sources blamed indiscipline on other factors. For instance, some church leaders and others blamed mixed-sex schools. Other explanations for indiscipline also occasionally appeared, as in a letter to the *SN* calling for more corporal punishment of students under 18: Ignatius Mwenda Ngore, "Why We Have Student Unrest," *SN*, 25 Aug. 1991, p. 10. International reports emphasizing the discipline issue include three stories submitted to Reuters on 22 July 1991 by Manoah Esipisu: "Kenyan Police Say Arrests Completed at Murder School," Reuters, 22 July 1991, NEXIS; "Officials Suspend All Boys in Kenyan Rape and Murder School," Reuters, 22 July 1991, NEXIS; and "Death and Rape at School Force Kenya to Look at Education Crisis," Reuters, 22 July 1991, NEXIS. The third story is the most detailed, discussing the "deeper roots" of indiscipline in poor management, unqualified staff, and autocratic disciplinary styles. The story's sources are both named and unnamed educational and government officials. Also, drugs are discussed as a factor.

14. The best example of an international story that blames incompetent administrators is David Chazen, "Kenya's Social Tensions," AFP, 16 July 1991, NEXIS. Editorials focusing on administrative incompetence include: "Kizito Tragedy: President's Decision Wins the Day," *SS*, 21 July 1991, p. 8; Robert Otani, "Lessons from Kizito," *KT*, 18 July 1991, p. 6; "Order to School Heads Timely," *S*, 15 Aug. 1991, p. 8; and Masoud Salim Mazrui, "St. Kizito Incident Calls for Revision of Education Policy," *S*, 20 Aug. 1991, p. 9. The three features emphasizing administrative incompetence which appeared the weekend following the crime are: Athanas Tuiyot, "School Violence," *S*, 20 July 1991, pp. 2–3; Mwicigi Njoroge, "Seeking the Roots," *KT*, 20 July 1991, 18; Wamahiu Muya, "Why Strikes and St. Kizito Tragedy Had to Happen," *SN*, 21 July 1991, pp. VII, X, XV. Stories on the coverage of Moi's team include, e.g., Ngomo wa Kuria, "Riots Caused by Heads at Schools, Team Told," *S*, 20 Aug. 1991, p. 5.

15. Most frequent spelling in press accounts. Other spellings: Kithera and Kathure. Note that Mrs. Kithira was the deputy to the headmaster. In press accounts she was sometimes described as the deputy to Laiboni, but more frequently as deputy headmistress.

16. "St. Kizito Headteacher Was 'Inexperienced,'" *DN*, 24 July

1991, p. 28. The quote is from Imanene Imathiu, "St. Kizito: KNUT Protests Sacking," *DN*, 14 Dec. 1991, p. 28.

17. For a good example of an inexperienced headmaster story quoting Karauri, see Raphael Kahaso, "Tragedy that Shocked All," *S*, 18 July 1991, p. 21. Concerned Parent, "Dialogue Is the Answer," *S*, 20 July 1991, p. III. The quote from Mr. Kibe is from Muya, "Why strikes," *SN*, 21 July 1991, p. VII.

18. "Why This Beastly Student Behavior?," *S*, p. 8. Chazen, "Kenya's Social Tensions," NEXIS. Three later international stories say that "authorities" blamed the incident on drug-taking and alcohol consumption by the students with no specific sources given. A likely source was this AFP copy, and/or a Reuters story by Esipisu, "Death and Rape," NEXIS. These three stories are: "39 Students Arrested, 265 Suspended," AFP, 22 July 1991, NEXIS; "39 Boys Held in Kenya after Dormitory Rampage," *Vancouver Sun*, 23 July 1991, NEXIS; and "39 Boys Arrested in Dorm Rampage," *The Ottawa Citizen*, 23 July 1991, NEXIS.

19. The minister of education, Mr. Peter Oloo Aringo's early statements appear in two stories: Imathiu, "71 Girls Raped," *DN*, 17 July 1991, p. 1; Njoroge, "Aringo: Plotters Responsible," *KT*, p. 1.

20. Murigi Macharia, "Kizito: Moi Warns Papers . . . Don't Use Tragedy to Incite Schools," *KT*, 24 July 1991, p. 2. Much briefer summaries of Moi's concerns and warning were published in "President Cautions Papers over Kizito," *S*, 24 July 1991, p. 13, and "St. Kizito: President Cautions Papers," *DN*, 24 July 1991, p. 1.

21. Otani, "Lessons from Kizito," *KT*, p. 8; Karanja, "Kizito: Are We Qualified," *SI*, pp. 6–7. The second opinion piece directly criticizes Mr. Aringo.

22. "Doctors Link Meru Tragedy to Stress," *DN*, 20 July 1991, p. 2.

23. Stories that quote prominent leaders blaming 8-4-4 include: Tuiyot, "School Violence," *S*, pp. 2–3; Grithuku Gracheru, "Riots: The Jobs Factor," *S*, 14 Aug. 1991, p. 3; "8-4-4 Expensive for Parents," *S*, 24 Aug. 1991, p. 5; Muya, "Why Strikes," *SN*, pp. 7–10, 15; Michael Njuguna, "Diocese Urges 8-4-4 Review," *DN*, 20 Aug. 1991, p. 3. Letters connecting the crime to 8-4-4 include: Bobby Kiama, "School Murder, Rape in Focus," *KT*, 20 July 1991, pp. 18, 19; J. Clifton, "An Idea to Ease the Workload," *DN*, 22 July 1991, p. 7; David K. Wang'ombe, David K. Maigiro, Mwangi Kanunda, "The 8-4-4 Factor in Schools' Unrest," 3 letters, *DN*, 26 July 1991, p. 7. The article attributing stress to meningitis is Irungu Ndirangu, "A Country Grap-

ples with the Aftermath of Gross Student Indiscipline . . . Could This Tragedy Have Been Averted?," *SN*, 21 July 1991, pp. VIII–IX.

24. Mwicigi Njoroge, "Mixed Schools Now Appear Untenable," *KT*, 17 Aug. 1991, p. 21.

25. Sanday, "Silencing the Feminine," Levinson, "Family Violence."

26. This was the case in the New York jogger rape, where the victim was white (and upper class) and her assailants were black (and working class). It was also the case in New Bedford, Mass. barroom rape, where the Portuguese community in which the incident occurred felt maligned by the reporting. Benedict, *Virgin or Vamp.*

27. Riithi, "Another St. Kizito shocker," *KT*, pp. 1, 7.

28. Muya, "Why Strikes," *SN*, pp. VII, X, XV.

29. Ndirangu, "A Country Grapples," SN. p. VIII. As noted previously, the spelling of the headmaster's name varies in press accounts. Though Laiboni is the most frequent spelling, Laibon, Laibun and Laibuni also appear. For background information on the Igembe-Tigania land dispute, see Goldsmith, "Symbiosis and Transformation," pp. 80–82.

30. Imanene Imathiu, "St. Kizito Dormitory 'Built on Haunted Site,'" *DN*, 17 Dec. 1991, p. 20.

31. The use of the subculture of violence defense in the hearings was reported in a lengthy *SN* feature by Ngugi wa Mbugua, "St. Kizito: A Kenyan Nightmare that Won't Go Away," 21 June 1992, pp. 4–5. See also Imanene Imathiu, "Officer Cites 'Kizito Jealousy,'" *SN*, 17 May 1992, p. 5, for a reference to Francis Apollos's testimony. This line of defense was also reported in international stories, such as Schofield, "Kenya: New Name But Old Values," 13 July 1992, *The Age* (Melbourne), NEXIS.

32. Karanja, "Are We Qualified," *ST*, p. 7. Mr. Apollos has a master's degree in criminology from the University of Cardiff in Britain, according to Jane Perlez, "Kenyans Do Some Soul-Searching after the Rape of 71 Schoolgirls," *New York Times*, 29 July 1991, p. A1.

33. Riithi, "Another St. Kizito Shocker," *KT*, p. 1, 7. According to the Karanja editorial (Karanja, "Are We Qualified," *ST*, p. 7), Riithi had written a *ST* feature published on 7 July 1991 (prior to the St. Kizito crime) about Mr. Apollos' research on Meru violence. Hence, Karanja's editorial quite directly encouraged further reports by Riithi, linking a "sub-culture of violence" with St. Kizito. In discussing Riithi's story, I use the spellings in the story. The spellings of the

headmaster's and headmistress's names vary in different stories and publications.

34. Ibid., p. 1.

35. Ibid., p. 7.

36. Ibid., p. 7.

37. Ibid., p. 7. Njoroge, "Aringo: Plotters Responsible," *KT*, pp. 1–2.

38. See chapter 2, subsection on "The Case," for a discussion of Meru values and the meaning of the circumcision ritual as described in Gideon S. Were and Simiyu Wandibba's 1988 edited collection. Although never accompanied by critical, comparative or in-depth analysis, several published exceptions to the popular view that rape is culturally indigenous to Meru are worth noting. The most significant is a joint statement issued by two women's organizations (reported in all three local papers on 1 August 1991) that includes a strong dismissal of the view that violence against women is a part of "any culture in Kenya or anywhere." See e.g., Cecilia Kamau, "Family Violence: Women's Bodies Take up the Cudgel," *KT*, 1 Aug. 1991, pp. 1,2. Also Cecilia Kamau's report on an August memorial service paraphrases a woman from Meru rejecting the view that rape was commonplace and stating that those espousing such views are "just trying to subjugate women." "Befitting Memorial for St. Kizito Girls," *KT*, 15 Aug. 1991, p. 6. Three other exceptions: Irungu Ndirangu, "Shops, Schools Shut as Thousands Mourn," *DN*, 19 July 1991, pp. 1, 15, which quotes the area MP, Mr. Mathew Adams Karauri, stating that Tigania people revere life and that circumcision teaches respect for other people, not rape; also, Jane Perlez, "Kenyans Do Some Soul-Searching," p. A1. Perlez quotes Riithi's article and one of his sources, Mr. Appolos, at length. However, she also interviewed a life-long Meru resident with a different view, who stated that traditionally manhood was expressed in ways such as "being a good herdsman, being a good decision maker—you didn't have to rape a girl."

39. For example, in two separate stories, Riithi reports that one of the nineteen girls who died, Rose Laibon, was "confirmed" to be the daughter of the headmaster, James Laibon (names that Riithi also spelled as Laibun and Laibuni). Alex Riithi, "Kizito Boys Are Like Dogs, Karauri," *KT*, 19 July 1991, p. 3; Alex Riithi, "Watchman charged in Kizito rape, death cases," *KT*, 20 July 1991, pp. 1, 2. Yet

neither of the other two newspapers reports this relationship and the *Sunday Nation* disconfirms it in Imanene Imathiu, "Kizito: 20 More Boys Arrested," *SN*, 21 July 1991, pp. 1, 2. On 1 Apr. 1994, I spoke with a *Kenya Times* correspondent and acquaintance of Alex Riithi. This reporter characterized Riithi as a respected journalist with a reputation for being thorough, accurate, and hard-working. He pointed out that Philip Ochieng was difficult to work for and could be a tyrant, especially when Ochieng decided to focus on a particular issue. "I'd say he [Riithi] was probably 70 per cent accurate under the circumstances," according to this source. He pointed out that the Meru group has a reputation for temper and abusive behavior toward women, especially after circumcision. "But this is very controversial." He felt that Riithi must have been especially concerned about accuracy given that he was reporting an incident in his home area. He had explanations for Riithi's apparent inaccuracies. With regard to the different spellings of Laiboni, he said there are several acceptable spellings. With regard to the inaccurately reported relation between Rose Laibon and the headmaster, the reporter said Laibon is not a common name, and Riithi's sources may therefore have understandably assumed a relation. He also pointed out that competing papers often are eager to discredit each other, hence the quick *Sunday Nation* correction.

40. The headmaster's denial of his published statements was reported by the Kenya News Agency (KNA) on 29 July 1991 and used by the British Broadcasting Corporation, Summary of World Broadcasts, "Kenya 29 Boys Charged with Manslaughter Following School Deaths," 31 July 1991, BBC, NEXIS. Local uses of Riithi's account and quotes include "Making the Punishment Fit the Crime," *WR*, 26 July 1991, pp. 14–16; and "Sexism in Kenya," *WR*, 9 Aug. 1991, pp. 4–20. Early international reports that use this story include "Rape Was Common at Kenyan School before Tragedy: Headmaster," AFP, 24 July 1991, NEXIS; "A Night of Madness," *Time*, 12 Aug. 1991, p. 43; Perlez, "Kenyans Do Some Soul-Searching," A1; Jane Perlez, "The Evil Men Do to Women in Kenya," *New York Times*, 4 Aug. 1991, p. A4; Sheryl McCarthy, "Cavemen Try Taking Women Back in Time: The Stone Age," *Newsday*, 31 July 1991, News section, p. 8; "Women and Violence—Kenya," *Women's International Network News* 4 (autumn 1991): 37–41. International stories after August 1991 that quote Riithi's story include: Lori Heise,

"When Women Are Prey: Around the World Rape Is Common-place—and the Victims Can't Fight Back," *Washington Post*, 8 Dec. 1991, p. C1; and Susan Okie, "The Boys 'Only Wanted to Rape Them,'" *Washington Post*, 17 Feb. 1993, p. A24.

41. For a discussion of Western stereotypes of Africa and Africans, see, e.g., Jo Ellen Fair, "War, Famine and Poverty: Race in the Construction of Africa's Media Image," *Journal of Communication Inquiry*, 17 (1993):5-22. See also Beverly G. Hawk's edited collection: *Africa's Media Image* (New York: Praeger, 1992).

42. International examples include Perlez, "Kenyans Do Some Soul-Searching," p. A1; Perlez, "Evil Men Do," p. 4; McCarthy, "Cavemen," p. 8; Heise, "When Women Are Prey," p. C1; Okie, "The Boys 'Only Wanted to Rape Them,'" p. A24; "Perspectives," *Newsweek*, 12 Aug. 1991, p. 15; "NOW Chapter Issues 'Turkey of the Year' Awards," UPI, Regional news (Illinois), 12 Nov. 1991.

43. Heise, "When Women Are Prey," p. C1; Timothy Dwyer, "Kenyans Haunted by Girls' Deaths," *Chicago Tribune*, 18 Aug. 1991, News section, p. 25; Benedict, 198–204.

44. McCarthy, "Cavemen," p. 8.

45. John Fiske, "Television: Polysemy and Popularity." *Critical Studies in Mass Communication* 3 (1986): 392.

46. "St. Kizito: 4 Girls Had Sex, Court Told," *S*, 11 Jan. 1992, p. 3; Imathiu, "Officer Cites 'Kizito Jealousy,'" *SN*, p. 5.

47. Irungu Ndirangu, "Death Dormitory Moves Moi to Tears," *DN*, 17 July 1991, p. 1. For an example of a story connecting mixed schools with indiscipline, see Njoroge, "Mixed Schools," *KT*, p. 21.

48. Ndirangu, "A Country Grapples," *SN*, pp. VIII–IX.

49. Muya, "Why Strikes," *SN*, p. xv.

50. Njoroge, "Mixed Schools," *KT*, p. 21.

51. P. S. Wanjala, "Get Rid of Mixed Schools," *DN*, 22 July 1991, p. 7.

52. Ndirangu, "Shops, Schools Shut," *DN*, p. 1. I note that while undoubtedly Kenyans throughout the country agreed with Mungatia (as indicated in citations to follow), it is likely he was indeed reflecting a view prevalent in Meru District, especially among elders. See, e.g., A. Kimokoti, "Education and Social Training," p. 139, 142.

53. Otani, "Lessons from Kizito," *KT*, p. 6, Musungu, "St. Kizito: Counseling," p. 7. (Other letters that call for an end to mixed schools for the same reason include Mazrui, "St. Kizito Incident," *S*, p. 9; and

Wanjala, "Get Rid of Mixed Schools," *DN*, p. 7.) A school watchman stated in court that "Boys and girls at St. Kizito Secondary School used to misbehave by holding each other whenever lights went off during their studies" ("St. Kizito: Mischief Alleged," *S*, 10 Dec. 1991, p. 4). Joe Ombuor, "Girls Transferred for Safety," *DN*, 30 May 1992, p. 14. Jane Some, Marianne King'ori, and James Wahome, "Kenyans React Angrily as They Urge for a Permanent Solution," *SN*, 21 July 1991, pp. VII–IX.

54. Ombour, "Girls Transferred for Safety," *DN*, p. 14; "Sexism in Kenya," *WR*, pp. 17–20; Perlez, "Evil men do," p. 4. One international feature story that focuses entirely on educational gender inequities in Kenya is: Gretchen Lang, "Elusive Dream; Poverty, Second-Class Status Keep Many Girls in Kenya from Pursuing Their Education," *The Dallas Morning News*, 6 May 1993, p. 39A. The story briefly mentions St. Kizito while noting that many parents fear for girls' safety and therefore prefer single-sex schools.

55. "Morals Never So Low," *DN*, p. 6. Examples of letters include: Karanja, "St. Kizito Is Society Problem," *DN*, p. 7; Pio Ciampa, S.J., "Kizito: Society Should Instil Morality in Youth," *KT*, 31 July 1991, p. 7; Robin Taabu, "Catholics Must Learn to Fight Evil," *KT*, 6 Aug. 1991, p. 7; and S. Moses Smith, "Use Chaplains for Moral Uprightness," *S*, 31 July 1991, p. 9.

56. Muya, "Why Strikes," *SN*, p. xv.

57. "8-4-4 Expensive for Parents," *S*, 24 Aug. 1991, p. 5.

58. Imanene Imathiu, "St. Kizito Students Suspended, 39 Held," *DN*, 22 July 1991, pp. 1–2; Michael Oongo, "Bishop Calls for St. Kizito Closure," *KT*, 22 July 1991, p. 4.

59. Ciampa, "Kizito: Society Should," *KT*, p. 7.

60. Asma Mohamed Abdel Halim, "Tools of Suppression," in *Gender Violence and Women's Human Rights in Africa*, ed. by Center for Women's Global Leadership (New Brunswick, N.J.: Center for Women's Global Leadership, Douglas College, 1994), 21–29.

61. A good example is the William Kennedy Smith trial. The victim did not want to be named, but once she was named by tabloids, other papers followed suit.

62. See Benedict, 252–53, 254. With regard to the destigmatization argument, it may also be countered that it is not the media's role to decide that individual victims will carry social burdens for the rest of us by helping to change society's prejudices (Carolyn Stewart Dyer, personal communication, Sept. 5, 1995.)

63. Many stories and photos name female rape victims. Even victims who were not explicitly identified with rape would likely be presumed raped by readers as "St. Kizito" and "rape" quickly became closely associated in the minds of Kenyans, and "Kizito" even became a metaphor for rape in popular culture. In the international press naming is not an issue as no victims or assailants were ever named. (An exception, not included in my sample, is a BBC Summary of World Broadcasts report that names two boys charged with the crime: "Kenya: 29 Boys Charged.") However, some photos of unnamed victims were used, whereas photos of the assailants were never used. For instance, AP photos of unnamed victims accompany the following stories: Perlez, "Kenyans Do Some Soul-Searching," p. A1; Perlez, "Evil Men Do," p. A4; and Dwyer, "Kenyans Haunted by Girls' Deaths," p. 25.

64. It is impossible to determine with certainty from NEXIS whether photographs accompanied international stories published during the first two days after the incident. No photographs are noted, however.

65. "The Meru Tragedy," *WR*, 19 July 1991, pp. 5–13.

66. Riithi, "Another St. Kizito Shocker," *KT*, pp. 1, 7. It should be noted that the worker quoted is Mercy Tharamba, a former student who had been given a kiosk by a teacher who reportedly had made her pregnant. The boys' resentment of her privileged situation is mentioned in early reports as one of several catalysts for the crime.

67. Laws of Kenya, Chapter 141, *The Children and Young Persons Act, rev. ed.* (Nairobi: Government Printer, 1972), section 5, p. 8. See also the *Weekly Review*, "Making the Punishment Fit the Crime," 26 July 1991, pp. 14–16, which summarizes this and related laws.

68. Imanene Imathiu, "Kizito: 20 More Boys Arrested," *SN*, 21 July 1991, pp. 1–2. Imanene Imathiu, "St. Kizito Tragedy: 29 Boys Charged," *DN*, 30 July 1991, p. 1; "St. Kizito Tragedy: Boy Denies Charge," *DN*, 7 Aug. 1991, p. 28; Imanene Imathiu, "Nine St. Kizito Boys Are Freed by Court," *DN*, 8 Aug. 1991, p. 28.

69. Imathiu, "Kizito: 20 More Boys Arrested," *SN*, p. 2. Imathiu, "St. Kizito Tragedy: 29 Boys Charged," *DN*, p. 28. Imathiu, "Nine St. Kizito Boys," *DN*, p. 28.

70. Imanene Imathiu, "30 Kizito Boys 'In Thugs Den,'" *DN*, 13 Aug. 1991, p. 4; "Kizito Court Petitioned," *KT*, 14 Aug. 1991, p. 4; Victor Nzomo, "Kizito: Plea for Bail Rejected," *S*, 14 Aug. 1991, p. 2; "Court to Visit Kizito Schoolboys in Prison," *DN*, 14 Aug. 1991, p. 32.

71. I am not necessarily challenging the validity or the newsworthiness of information in the *DN*'s sympathetic stories cited here. My concern is rather the *meaning* of this information, alongside its absence in other publications and the *DN*'s unwillingness to name assailants. Examples of these September stories include Imathiu: "Kizito Boys Sent to Different Schools," *DN*, p. 4; "43 St. Kizito Boys Report to Kangaru ," *DN*, p. 4. Imanene Imathiu, "St. Kizito boys Are Ill—Lawyer," *DN*, 10 Oct. 1991, p. 32. Imanene Imathiu, "4 St. Kizito Boys Jailed for Manslaughter," *DN*, 19 Feb. 1992, pp. 1, 6.

72. "St. Kizito: Four Boys Jailed," *DN*, 18 Mar. 1992, p. 5. This story indicates continued denial of the convicted assailants' culpability by focusing primarily on quotes from Meru probation officer and criminologist Mr. Apollos, stating that the killings were "accidental" and blame should be directed at school administrators and drug-sellers.

73. Imanene Imathiu, "St. Kizito: Nurse Took Body Specimens," *DN*, 5 Dec. 1991, p. 4; Imanene Imathiu, "Former Prefect at St. Kizito Testifies," *DN*, 3 Apr. 1992, p. 13.

74. "The Meru Tragedy,"*WR*, 19 July 1991, p. 9.

75. Riithi, "Another St. Kizito Shocker," *KT*, p. 1, 7.

76. Alex Riithi, "St. Kizito: Nine Boys Bonded," *KT*, 8 Aug. 1991, p. 3; "Nine Kizito Boys Are Bonded," *WR*, 23 Aug. 1991, pp. 13–14; "Warrant for St. Kizito Boy," *KT*, 2 Jan. 1992, p. 5; Alex Riithi, "Four St. Kizito Boys Imprisoned," *KT*, 19 Feb. 1992, pp. 1, 3.

77. Victor Nzomo, "St. Kizito Tragedy: 29 Boys in Court," *S*, 30 July 1991, pp. 1, 2.

78. For instance, in 1991 the *Sunday Standard* launched a slick Sunday entertainment magazine, called *Now*. I note also that President Moi's son, Mark Too, had an involvement in the *Standard*, as deputy chairman of Lonrho East Africa. Later, Too became chairman of the new government-affiliated company that purchased the *Standard* from Lonrho. See Wachiria, "Kenya-Media: President's Men Acquire."

79. Esther Kamweru, "Rape: Violation of Women's Rights," *SS*, 26 Apr. 1992, Features, pp. IV–V.

80. Victor Nzomo, "St. Kizito: 9 Boys Bonded to Keep Peace," *S*, 8 Aug. 1991, p. 1; Victor Nzomo, "Four St. Kizito Boys Jailed for Four Years," *S*, 19 Feb. 1992, pp. 1–2; "Kizito Boys Get 16 Years," *S*, 18 Mar. 1992, p. 12.

81. Stamp, "Burying Otieno."

82. Laws of Kenya, chapter 141, section 15, p. 11.

83. Ndirangu and Imathiu, "Moi Orders Investigation," *DN*, p. 1; "Rampaging Boys Hide in Bush," *S*, pp. 1, 13; Victor Nzomo, "39 Riotous Students Arrested . . . 265 St. Kizito's Boys Suspended," *S*, 22 July 1991, p. 1; Riithi, "29 Kizito Boys Deny," *KT*, p. 1; McCarthy, "Cavemen," p. 8; "Kenyan Riot Boys in Court," NEXIS; "Meru Tragedy," *WR*, p. 1; Rogoncho, "Kizito Victims' Memorial Date Set," *SN*, p. 5; Kariuki, "St. Kizito: Students Declared Martyrs," *SS*, p. 12.

84. I only note a label once per story, even though it may have been used many times, as in the case of "boys," "girls," or "students." Labels for the dead victims (most often referred to as "the dead") were not counted unless they included survivors as well. A possible exception was "martyr," which primarily referred to the dead. I looked at all stories in the three Nairobi dailies for the first six weeks and twenty-one international reports, i.e., the twenty-one reports that I obtained from LEXIS/NEXIS in August of 1993.

85. For an example of the victim of circumstances argument, see Imathiu, "30 Kizito Boys 'In Thugs Den,'" *DN*, p. 4. Stories referring to assailants over 18 as "boys" include: Riithi, "Four St. Kizito Boys Imprisoned," *KT*, pp. 1, 3; Imathiu, "4 St. Kizito Boys Jailed for Manslaughter," *DN*, pp. 1, 6; Nzomo, "Four St. Kizito Boys Jailed for Four Years," *S*, pp. 1, 2; "Kizito Boys Get 16 Years," *S*, p. 12.

86. Morals Were Never So Low in Schools," *DN*, 16 July 1991, p. 6; "Why This Beastly Student Behavior?" *S*, 16 July 1991, p. 8; Macharia, "Meru Villagers Mourn Their Dead," *KT*, p. 1.

87. Of the three local papers, the *Kenya Times* most frequently used labels like "psychotic," "insane," "beastly," and "criminal." Benedict suggests that in the New York jogger gang rape, this sort of language—especially the concept of "wilding"—suggests racist stereotypes and fears. Benedict, *Virgin or Vamp*, 198–204. Given that the *Kenya Times* allocated the most space to the subculture of violence idea, one might speculate that this language is not completely accidental.

88. A *Daily Nation* story by Imanene Imathiu was headlined "Kizito Boys Wanted to See 'Their Wives,'" *DN*, p. 11 Dec. 1991, p. 24, and indicates that the St. Kizito boys frequently referred to the girls as their "wives," connoting sexual property. This is also consistent with the patriarchal myth that rape does not occur in marriage. The same information was reported in "St. Kizito: Mischief Alleged," *S*, 10 Dec. 1991, p. 4.

Chapter 4. Feminist Framing

1. Both quotes in this paragraph are from "Boys' Parents Get Ultimatum," p. 2. According to "Meru Villagers Mourn Their Dead," *KT*, p. 2, others who attended the meeting where the decision was made to transfer the girls were Mr. Tom Sitima, the chief inspector of schools, Mr. Sammy Kyungu, the eastern provincial education officer, and Mr. Julius Mbogo, the Meru police chief. Transfer stories are: Imanene Imathiu, "Girls from St. Kizito Transferred," *DN*, 25 July 1991, p. 32; Alex Riithi, "Now St. Kizito Girls Join Other Schools," *KT*, 25 July 1991, p. 3.

2. Raphael Kahaso, "Ordeal at Kizito," *S*, 18 July 1991, p. 20.

3. Most notable is a letter by Mrs. Margaret Njoroge, which appears in both *S* ("Girls Should Remain at St. Kizito," 24 July 1991, p. 9) and *KT* ("Stop Other Kizito Tragedies," 29 July 1991, p. 7). Njoroge's *KT* letter is one of three under the same headline.

4. Murigi Macharia and Julia Gichuhi, "Leave Kizito Girls Alone, Orders Moi," *KT*, 19 July 1991, pp. 1, 2; "Reconsider Kizito Girls' Transfer—Moi," *S*, 19 July 1991, pp. 1, 12; Imanene Imathiu, "Meru DC Puts off Transfer of Girls," *DN*, 20 July 1991, pp. 1, 2.

5. Imanene Imathiu, "Kizito Boys Sent to Different Schools," *DN*, 20 Sept. 1991, p. 4; Alex Riithi, "St. Kizito Students to Be Shifted," *KT*, 18 Sept. 1991, p. 5; "43 St. Kizito Boys Report to Kangaru High School," *DN*, 18 Sept. 1991, p. 4.

6. Mothers In Action visited the survivors' schools and facilitated some group and individual counseling sessions. This was first reported in the Kenyan press in a story by Christine Mpaka, "Burying Memory of Night of Madness," *SN*, 26 July 1992, sec. Lifestyle, p. 5. It is noteworthy that Michele Landsberg reported Mothers in Action's counseling efforts in her October *Toronto Star* column, "School Attack Inspires Action by Women of Kenya," *Toronto Star*, 12 Oct. 1991, p. F1. The *SN* (Mbugua, "St. Kizito: A Kenyan Nightmare") reported that sixty boys and fifty-nine girls took university-qualifying exams. In the past, the girls and boys had competed fairly equally; yet on these exams six boys and no girls performed at a level to qualify for university entrance. Also, an earlier *KT* story reported how well the boys were doing academically, with no mention of the girls (Alex Riithi, "St. Kizito Revisited," *KT*, 8 Apr. 1992, pp. 14, 15).

7. Oketch Kendo, "An Example of Violence against Women," *S*, 18 July 1991, p. 21.

8. Hilary Ng'weno, "Letter from the Editor," *WR*, 19 July 1991, p. 1.

9. Mkanju, "Ministry Should Act Promptly over Children," *SN*, 21 July 1991, p. xii.

10. Kamau, "Family Violence," *KT*, p. 1. Exceptions include Imathiu, "St. Kizito Students Suspended," *DN*, pp. 1–2. This story quotes Rev. Njoya, a Presbyterian clergyman who stated that the Kizito girls are "not martyrs but outright victims of our male chauvinism and political injustice." Another exception is Wahome Mutahi, "Society Is to Blame for Rising School Violence," *DN*, 22 July 1991, p. 6, which suggests that the problem is grounded partly in the family, which shows boys "that men should be men and treat women like rubbish." This, however, is a minor part of a rather rambling opinion piece that also blames rising violence in schools on women in Nairobi who don't spend enough time with their children.

11. Anjili, "Don't Exploit Women—Nuns," *S*, p. 14; "Women Want More Posts," *DN*, 22 July 1991, p. 3; "Women to Discuss Child Abuse," *DN*, 26 July 1991, p. 3.

12. Kamau, "Family Violence," *KT*, p. 1-2. "Women Call for Family Courts," *DN*, 1 Aug. 1991, p. 3; Kihu Irimu, "Women in Plea over Violence," *S*, 1 Aug. 1991, p. 4; Charles Kulundu, "Violence: Women Appeal to Government," *KT*, 3 Aug. 1991, p. 15.

13. Kamau, "Family Violence," *KT*, p. 1–2.

14. Alphonse Mung'ahu, "mywo Call for End of Violence against Women," *SS*, 11 Aug. 1991, p. 3; David Rogoncho, "Kizito Victims' Memorial Date Set," *SN*, 11 Aug. 1991, p. 5; "Memorial for Kizito Girls Held," *KT*, 14 Aug. 1991, p. 2; Cecilia Kamau, "Befitting Memorial for St. Kizito Girls," *KT*, 15 Aug. 1991, p. 6; Emman Omari, "Service in Memory of St. Kizito Girls," *DN*, 14 Aug. 1991, p. 3; "St. Kizito Girls Are Remembered," *S*, 15 Aug. 1991, p. 5.

15. Rasna Warah, "Rape: Why the Apathy?," *SN*, 4 Aug. 1991, p. 8.

16. Martha Mbugguss, "This Violence Should Stop Now," *DN*, 14 Aug. 1991, p. 8; Kidji Nduku, "Kenyan Women Are Angry," *S*, 7 Aug. 1991, pp. 17, 20; "Sexism in Kenya," *WR*, 9 Aug. 1991, pp. 4-20.

17. Ms. Anyanzwa's first name is spelled as both "Fatma" and "Fatuma" in media reports. Examples of stories that report on her

activism include: "Anti-Rape Crusaders to Launch Body," *KT*, 12 Oct. 1991, p. 4; Kathryn Kahiko, "A Lifeline for Rape Victims," *KT*, 26 Oct. 1991, p. 14; "Anti-Rape Body Now Registered," *KT*, 4 Feb. 1992, p. 5; Murigi Macharia, "The Ugly Subject of Rape and How Kenyan Law Sees It," *ST*, 16 Feb. 1992, p. 19; Richard Keya, "Anti-Rape Group Protests," *S*, 23 Feb. 1992, p. 6; "Rape: Law Reform Urged," *KT*, 23 Feb. 1992, p. 3; "The Anti-Rape Organization," *WR*, 28 Feb. 1992, p. 16; "Let Courts Settle Rape Cases," *S*, 1 Mar. 1992, p. 4; "Chiefs Told to Keep off Rape Cases," *ST*, 1 Mar. 1992, p. 5; "Establish Anti-Rape Unit, Urges Anyanzwa," *KT*, 4 Mar. 1992, p. 3; "Establish Anti-Rape Unit, Kilonzo Urged," *S*, 19 Mar. 1992, p. 3; "Rape: Police Praised," *S*, 21 Mar. 1992, p. 5; Ruben Olita, "Rape: 'Violation of Human Rights,'" *S*, 19 Apr. 1992, p. 4; "Rape: Woman Petitions Judges," *S*, 20 Apr. 1992, p. 13; Rasna Warah, "Are Women Responsible for Rape?" *SS*, 3 Mar. 1992, sec. Now Magazine, pp. 2–3; "Rape: Prayers Planned," *S*, 1 June 1992, p. 5; Alfred Omondi, "Police 'Dropped Rape Case,'" *S*, 16 June 1992, p. 3; "Prayers for Rape Victims Proposed," *DN*, 11 July 1992, p. 5; "St. Kizito Prayers Today," *S*, 12 July 1992, p. 4.

Stories reporting on the activism of Mothers in Action include: "Women Rap MP over Rape Story," *ST*, 15 Sept. 1991, p. 4; "Women's Organization Hits at Leitich over Rape Utterances," *SS*, 15 Sept. 1991, p. 3; Mwicigi Njoroge, "City Rape Suspect Held," *KT*, 22 Feb. 1992, pp. 1, 17; Mpaka, "Burying Memory," *SN*, p. 5.

An example of an existing organization that shifted attention to gender violence is the Kenya chapter of the African Association for Women's Research and Development (AAWORD), which made a statement in September 1991 announcing an analysis of the St. Kizito crime, among other priorities. "Body Vows to Fight for Rights of Women," *KT*, 6 Sept. 1991, p. 3. Additionally, the Women's Bureau of Kenya published "A Guide to Women of Kenya on Rape and the Legal Process," which resulted in publicity, e.g., "Violence against Women Needs Attention," *KT*, 16 Jan. 1992, p. 15. In other stories, the chair of the Kenya Nurses Association condemned an incident of police brutality against a woman. "KNA Boss Condemns Violence on Women," *KT*, 20 Mar. 1992, p. 5. And in a *Kenya Times* story, the chair of the Kenya Business and Professional Women's Club denounced the sexual abuse of a housegirl at the hands of her employer. Evans Luseno, "Mugo Rails at Brutal Mistreatment of Girl," *KT*, 27 Mar. 1992, p. 7. The new legal aid clinic is described in Margareta wa Gacheru, "Legal Shelter for Terrorized Girls, Mothers," *SN*, 3 May 1992, Lifestyle sec., p. 5.

18. The Nakuru KANU chairman's remarks are reported in "Women's Organisation Hits at Leitich," p. 3. The Cardinal made his "scanty dressing" remarks on Easter Sunday, 19 April 1992 at the Holy Family Basilica, Nairobi. Ms. Fatuma Anyanzwa of the Kenya Anti-Rape Organization and others immediately challenged his statement. See "Otunga's Rape Quip Slammed," *KT*, 21 Apr. 1992, p. 2; Mwangi Githahu, "Inviting Rape: The Cardinal's Quip on Women's Dressing Sparks Debate on Rape," *ST*, 26 Apr. 1992, sec. Focus, pp. 9, 10; Esther Kamweru, "Rape: Violation of Women's Rights," *SS*, pp. iv–v; Maina Muiri, "Scanty Dressing and Rape," *S*, 17 Apr. 1992, pp. 14–15.

19. Kamau, "Family Violence," *KT*, p. 1; "Sexism in Kenya," *WR*, pp. 4–20. For a report of the arrest of Ms. Anyanzwa, see Horace Awori, "Kenya: Detained Anti-Rape Activist Remains Defiant," Inter Press Service, 28 Sept. 1993, NEXIS.

20. July and August 1991 international stories with feminist themes that also use quotes from or refer to Riithi's "Another St. Kizito Shocker" include: Perlez, "Kenyans Do Some Soul-Searching," p. A1; Perlez, "Evil Men Do," p. A4; McCarthy, "Cavemen."

21. "Rape and Murder at Kenyan Catholic Boarding School in Meru," *Women's International Network News*, 17:4 (Aug. 1991): 37; Perlez, "Kenyans Do Some Soul-Searching," p. A1; Perlez, "Evil Men Do," p. A4; Kamau, "Family Violence."

22. Landsberg, "School attack." Landsberg travelled to Kenya to lead a UNICEF-sponsored workshop on the history of feminism and also interviewed several Kenyan feminists, quoted in her column. Michele Landsberg, personal communication, 13 Mar. 1996.

23. Riithi, "Another St. Kizito Shocker," *KT*, 1, 7; Heise, "When Women Are Prey," p. C1; Okie, "The Boys 'Only Wanted to Rape Them,'" p. A24. Heise's story leads with St. Kizito but addresses rape globally, and Okie's story mentions St. Kizito as a part of a broader discussion about gender violence in Kenya. Inter Press Service stories mentioning St. Kizito and emphasizing feminist activism include: Horace Awori, "Kenya: Castrate, Hang, Flog Rapists, Women Say," Inter Press Service, 18 March 1993, NEXIS; and Awori, "Kenya: Detained Anti-Rape Activist Remains Defiant," Inter Press Service, 28 September 1993, NEXIS.

24. e.g., Gitlin, 28; Tuchman, *Making News*, 139.

Chapter 5. Conclusions

1. Tuchman, *Making News*, e.g., pp. 133–34.
2. Landsberg, "School Attack."
3. Fiske, "Television," 1986, p. 403.
4. Benedict, especially the Conclusion, 251–66. See Steeves, "Sharing Information in Kenya," for a discussion of communication and information policy in Kenya.

Bibliography

Abuoga, John Baptist, and Absalom Aggrey Mutere. *The History of the Press in Kenya*. Nairobi: African Council on Communication Education, 1988.

Adagala, Esther, and Wambui Kiai. "Folk, Interpersonal and Mass Media: The Experience of Women of Africa." In *Women Empowering Communication: A Resource Book on Women and Globalization of Media*, ed. Margaret Gallagher and Lilia Quindoza-Santiago, 11–35. New York: Women's International Tribune Centre, 1994.

Akong'a, Joshua. "Social Stratification." In *Meru District Socio-Cultural Profile*, eds. Gidion S. Were and Simiyu Wandibba, 93–109. Nairobi, Kenya: Government of Kenya and University of Nairobi (Classic Printers & Stationers Ltd.), 1988.

Althusser, Louis. *Lenin and Philosophy and Other Essays*, translated by B. Brewster. London: New Left Books, 1971.

Amir, Menachem. *Patterns in Forcible Rape*. Chicago: Univ. of Chicago Press, 1971.

Amnesty International. *Women in Kenya: Repression and Resistance*. London: Amnesty International, 1995.

Anderson, Perry. "The Antinomies of Antonio Gramsci." *New Left Review* 100 (Nov. 1976–Jan. 1977): 5–78.

Baron, Larry, and Murray A. Straus. *Four Theories of Rape in American Society*. New Haven: Yale Univ. Press, 1989.

The Bibliography lists references cited other than newspaper stories. For press sources cited, see the Endnotes for each chapter. See also Appendix A for a list of news stories about St. Kizito published in the Kenyan and international press for the year following the crime.

Benedict, Helen. *Virgin or Vamp: How the Press Covers Sex Crimes.* New York: Oxford Univ. Press, 1992.

Boserup, Ester. *Women's Role in Economic Development.* New York: St. Martin's Press, 1970.

Brownmiller, Susan. *Against Our Will: Men, Women, and Rape.* New York: Simon & Schuster, 1975.

Carrillo, Roxanna. *Battered Dreams: Violence against Women as an Obstacle to Development.* New York: UNIFEM, 1992.

Center for Women's Global Leadership. *Gender Violence and Women's Human Rights in Africa.* New Brunswick, N.J.: Center for Women's Global Leadership, Douglass College, 1994.

Chibnall, Steve. *Law-and-Order News.* London: Tavistock, 1977.

Cuklanz, Lisa M. "News Coverage of Ethnic and Gender Issues in the Big Dan's Rape Case." In *Feminist Media Studies in a Global Setting: Beyond Binary Contradictions and into Multicultural Spectrums,* ed. Angharad N. Valdivia, 145–62. Thousand Oaks, Calif.: Sage, 1995.

Darkwa, A. "Music and Dance Traditions." In *Meru District Socio-Cultural Profile,* eds. Gidion S. Were and Simiyu Wandibba, 165–90. Nairobi, Kenya: Government of Kenya and University of Nairobi (Classic Printers & Stationers Ltd.), 1988.

Dow, Bonnie. "Hegemony, Feminist Criticism and the Mary Tyler Moore Show." *Critical Studies in Mass Communication* 7 (1990): 261–74.

Ehrhart, Julie K., and Bernice R. Sandler. *Campus Gang Rape: Party Games?* Washington, D.C.: Project on the Status and Education of Women, 1985.

Ellis, Lee. *Theories of Rape: Inquiries into the Causes of Sexual Aggression.* New York: Hemisphere Publishing Corporation, 1989.

Entman, Robert M. "Framing: Toward Clarification of a Fractured Paradigm." *Journal of Communication* 43:4 (autumn 1993): 51–58.

Estrich, Susan. *Real Rape.* Cambridge, Mass.: Harvard University Press, 1985.

Fadiman, Jeffrey. *Oral Traditions of the Meru of the Mt. Kenya Region* (Athens: Ohio Univ. Press), 1982.

Fair, Jo Ellen. "War, famine and poverty: Race in the construction of Africa's media image." *Journal of Communication Inquiry* 17 (1993): 5–22.

Farstad, Elizabeth. "News Coverage of the New Bedford Rape Case." Master's thesis, University of Oregon, 1989.

Finn, G. "Taking Gender into Account in the 'Theatre of Terror': Violence, Media and the Maintenance of Male Dominance." *Canadian Journal of Women and the Law* 3:2 (1989–90): 375–94.

Fiske, John. "British Cultural Studies and Television." In *Channels of Discourse, Reassembled*, ed. Robert C. Allen, 284–326. Chapel Hill: Univ. of North Carolina Press, 1992.

Fiske, John. "Television: Polysemy and Popularity," *Critical Studies in Mass Communication* 3 (1986): 391–408.

Fortune, Marie Marshall. *Sexual Violence: The Unmentionable Sin.* New York: Pilgrim Press, 1983.

Gager, Nancy, and Cathleen Schurr. *Sexual Assault: Confronting Rape in America.* New York: Grosset & Dunlap, 1976.

Gallagher, Margaret. *Unequal Opportunities: The Case of Women and the Media.* Paris: The UNESCO Press, 1981.

———. "Women and Men in the Media." *Communication Research Trends* 12:1 (1992): 1–36.

Gans, Herbert. *Deciding What's News: A Study of CBS Evening News, NBC Nightly News, Newsweek, and Time.* New York: Vintage Books, 1980.

Geis, Gilbert. "Forcible Rape: An Introduction." In *Forcible Rape: The Crime, the Victim, and the Offender*, ed. Duncan Chappel, Robley Geis, and Gilbert Geis, 1–44. New York: Columbia Univ. Press, 1977.

———. "Group Sexual Assaults." *Medical Aspects of Human Sexuality* 5:5 (1971): 100–13.

Gitlin, Todd. *The Whole World Is Watching: Mass Media and the Making and Unmaking of the New Left.* Berkeley: Univ. of California Press, 1980.

Glasgow Media Group. *More Bad News.* London: Routledge & Kegan Paul, 1980.

Goffman, Erving. *Frame Analysis: An Essay on the Organization of Experience.* New York: Harper and Row, 1974.

Goldsmith, Paul. "Symbiosis and Transformation in Kenya's Meru District." Ph.D. dissertation, University of Florida, 1994.

Gordon, Margaret T., and Stephanie Riger. *The Female Fear.* New York: Free Press, 1989.

Goro, Victoria N., and Sophie A. Muluka-Lutta. "An Analysis of the Roles Portrayed by Women in Television Advertising: Nature and Extent of Sexism Present." Unpublished research paper, School of Journalism, University of Nairobi, 1991.

Gramsci, A. *Selections from the Prison Notebooks*, edited and translated by Q. Hoare and G. Nowell-Smith. New York: International Publishers, 1971.

Griffin, Susan. "Rape: The All-American Crime," *Ramparts* 10:3 (1971): 26–35.

Growth, A. Nicholas, with H. Jean Birnbaum. *Men Who Rape: The Psychology of the Offender*. New York: Plenum Press, 1979.

Hachten, William A. *The Growth of Media in the Third World: African Failures, Asian Successes*. Ames, Iowa: Iowa State Univ. Press, 1993.

Halim, Asma Mohamed Abdel. "Tools of Suppression." In *Gender Violence and Women's Human Rights in Africa*, ed. Center for Women's Global Leadership, 21–29. New Brunswick, N.J.: Center for Women's Global Leadership, Douglass College, 1994.

Hall, Stuart. "Encoding/Decoding." In *Culture, Media and Language: Working Papers in Cultural Studies*, ed. S. Hall, D. Hobson, A. Lowe, and P. Willis, 128–38. London: Hutchinson, 1980.

———. Introduction. In *Paper Voices: The Popular Press and Social Change, 1935–1965*, ed. A. C. H. Smith, 11–24. London: Chatto & Windus, 1975.

Hawk, Beverly G., ed. *Africa's Media Image*. New York: Praeger, 1992.

Heise, Lori L. *Fact Sheet on Gender Violence: A Statistics for Action Fact Sheet*. New York: IWTC/UNIFEM Resource Centre, 1992.

———. "Gender-Based Abuse: The Global Epidemic." In *Reframing Women's Health: Multidisciplinary Research and Practice*, ed. Alice J. Dan, 233–50. Thousand Oaks, Calif.: Sage, 1994.

Higgins, Lynn A., and Brenda A. Silver, eds. *Rape and Representation*. New York: Columbia Univ. Press, 1991.

Hirsch, Susan F. "Interpreting Media Representations of a 'Night of Madness': Law and Culture in the Construction of Rape Identities," *Law and Social Inquiry* 19(4) (1994): 1023–1058.

Jaggar, Allison. *Feminist Politics and Human Nature*. Sussex: The Harvester Press, 1983.

Kalule, H. "Marriage and Related Customs." In *Meru District Socio-Cultural Profile*, eds. Gidion S. Were and Simiyu Wandibba,

110–19. Nairobi, Kenya: Government of Kenya and University of Nairobi (Classic Printers & Stationers Ltd.), 1988.

Kenya Office of the Vice President and Ministry of Planning and National Development. *Meru District Development Plan 1994–96*. Nairobi: Kenya Office of the Vice President and Ministry of Planning and National Development, 1994.

Kimokoti, A. "Education and Social Training." In *Meru District Socio-Cultural Profile*, eds. Gidion S. Were and Simiyu Wandibba, 130–43. Nairobi, Kenya: Government of Kenya and University of Nairobi (Classic Printers & Stationers Ltd.), 1988.

Laws of Kenya, Chapter 63. *The Penal Code, rev. ed*. Nairobi: Government Printer, 1985.

Laws of Kenya, Chapter 141. *The Children and Young Persons Act, rev. ed*. Nairobi: Government Printer, 1972.

Lent, John. *Women and Mass Communication: An International Annotated Bibliography*. Westport, Conn.: Greenwood Press, 1991.

Levinson, David. *Family Violence in Cross-Cultural Perspective*. Newbury Park, Calif.: Sage, 1989.

MacKinnon, Catharine A. "Turning Rape into Pornography: Postmodern Genocide." *Ms.*, 4:1 (1993): 24–30.

Maja-Pearce, Adewale. "The Press in East Africa." *Index on Censorship* 21:7 (July/Aug. 1992): 50–73.

Manning, Peter K., and Betsy Cullum-Swan. "Narrative, Content, and Semiotic Analysis." In *Handbook of Qualitative Research*, ed. Norman K. Denzin and Yvonna S. Lincoln, 463–77. Thousand Oaks, Calif.: Sage, 1994.

Marshall, Catherine, and Gretchen B. Rossman. *Designing Qualitative Research*. Newbury Park, Calif.: Sage, 1989.

Mathu, G. "The Legal System." In *Meru District Socio-Cultural Profile*, eds. Gidion S. Were and Simiyu Wandibba, 120–29. Nairobi, Kenya: Government of Kenya and University of Nairobi (Classic Printers & Stationers Ltd.), 1988.

Meyers, Marian. "News of Battering." *Journal of Communication* 44:2 (1994): 47–63.

Mills, Kay. *A Place in the News*. New York: Dodd, Mead, 1988.

Mouffe, Chantal. "Hegemony and Ideology in Gramsci." In *Gramsci and Marxist Theory*, ed. Chantal Mouffe, 168–204. London: Routledge & Kegan Paul, 1979.

Mwangi, Wagaki. "Assessment of the Portrayal of Women in Kenyan Print Media, before, during and after the United Nations Decade for Women." Unpublished research paper, School of Journalism, University of Nairobi, 1991.

Nzomo, Maria. "The Impact of the Women's Decade on Policies, Programs and Empowerment of Women in Kenya." *Issue: A Journal of Opinion*, 17:2 (1989): 9–17.

Nzomo, Maria, and Kathleen Staudt. "Man-Made Political Machinery in Kenya: Political Space for Women?" In *Women and Politics Worldwide*, ed. Najma Chowdhury and Barbara Nelson, 416–35. New Haven, Conn.: Yale Univ. Press, 1994.

Obura, Anne. *Changing Images: Portrayal of Girls and Women in Kenyan Textbooks.* Nairobi, Kenya: Acts Press, 1991.

Ochieng, Philip. *I Accuse the Press: An Insider's View of the Media and Politics in Africa.* Nairobi: Initiatives Publishers, 1992.

Pathak, Zakia, and Rajeswari Sunder Rajan. "Shahbano." *Signs* 16:4 (1992): 808–45.

Pauley, John. "A Beginner's Guide to Doing Qualitative Research." *Journalism Monographs* 125 (Feb. 1991): 1–29.

Reissman, Catherine Kohler. *Narrative Analysis.* Newbury Park, Calif.: Sage, 1993.

Republic of Kenya, *Development Plan 1994–1996.* Nairobi: Government Printer, 1994.

———. Central Bureau of Statistics. *Statistical Abstract, 1990.* Nairobi: Government Printer, 1990.

Rozee-Koker, Patricia A., and Glenda C. Polk. "The Social Psychology of Group Rape." *Sexual Coercion & Assault* 1:2 (1986): 57–65.

Rugene, Catherine Njeri. "The Portrayal of Women in the Humour Columns of the Sunday Newspapers." Unpublished research paper, School of Journalism, University of Nairobi, 1991.

Ruigu, George M. *Women Employment in Kenya.* Nairobi, Kenya: Univ. of Nairobi, Institute for Development Studies, 1985.

Sanday, Peggy Reeves. *Fraternity Gang Rape: Sex, Brotherhood, and Privilege on Campus.* New York: New York Univ. Press, 1990.

———. "Silencing the Feminine." In *Rape: An Historical and Social Enquiry*, ed. Silvana Tomaselli and Roy Porter, 84–101. New York: Basil Blackwell, 1986.

Schuler, Margaret, ed. *Claiming Our Place: Working the Human Rights*

System to Women's Advantage. Washington, D.C.: Institute for Women, Law and Development, 1993.

———. ed. *Freedom from Violence: Women's Strategies from around the World.* New York: UNIFEM, 1992.

Stamp, Patricia. "Burying Otieno: The Politics of Gender and Ethnicity in Kenya." *Signs* 16:4 (1991): 808–45.

Staudt, Kathleen. *Agricultural Policy Implementation: A Case Study from Western Kenya.* West Hartford, Conn.: Kumarian Press, 1985.

Steeves, H. Leslie. "Creating Imagined Communities: Development Communication and the Challenge of Feminism." *Journal of Communication* 43:3 (summer 1993): 218–29.

———. "Feminist Theories and Media Studies." *Critical Studies in Mass Communication* 4:2 (1987): 95–135.

———. "Gender and Mass Communication in a Global Context." In *Women in Mass Communication, 2d ed.,* ed. P. Creedon, 32–60. Newbury Park, Calif.: Sage, 1993.

———. "Sharing Information in Kenya: Communication and Information Policy Considerations and Consequences for Rural Women," *Gazette,* 56 (1996): 157–81.

———. "Women, Rural Information Delivery, and Development in Sub-Saharan Africa." Michigan State University, Working Paper no. 212, 1990.

Steeves, H. Leslie, and Rebecca A. Arbogast. "Feminism and Communication in Development: Ideology, Law, Ethics, Practice." In *Progress in Communication Sciences,* vol. 11, ed. B. Dervin and U. Hariharan, 229–77. Norwood, N.J.: Ablex, 1993.

Stromquist, N. P. "Women and Literacy: Promises and Constraints." *Media Development* 1 (1990): 10–13.

Sunday, Suzanne R., and Ethel Tobach, eds. *Violence against Women: A Critique of the Sociobiology of Rape.* New York: Gordon Press, 1985.

Tomaselli, Silvana, and Roy Porter, eds. *Rape: An Historical and Social Enquiry.* New York: Basil Blackwell, 1986.

Tuchman, Gaye. *Making News: A Study in the Construction of Reality.* New York: The Free Press, 1978.

———. "Telling Stories." *Journal of Communication* 26:4 (Aug. 1976): 93–96.

UNESCO. *Communication in the Service of Women: A Report on Action and Research Programmes, 1980–1985.* Paris: UNESCO, 1985.

United Nations. *Report of the Fourth World Conference on Women.* Beijing, 4–15 Sept. 1995. Internet:http://www.igc.apc.org/womensnet/beijing/un/un.html.

United Nations. *World Media Handbook: Selected Country Profiles, 1995 Edition.* New York: U.N. Department of Public Information, 1995 (DP1/1614. Sales No. E.95.1.34).

United Nations. *The United Nations and the Advancement of Women, 1945–1996.* (The United Nations Blue Books Series, Volume VI, revised edition). New York: United Nations, 1996.

United Nations. *The World's Women 1995: Trends and Statistics.* New York: United Nations, 1995.

Vidich, Arthur J., and Stanford M. Lyman. "Qualitative Methods: Their History in Sociology and Anthropology." In *Handbook,* ed. N. K. Denzin and Y. S. Lincoln, 23-59. Thousand Oaks, Calif.: Sage, 1994.

Vogelman, Lloyd. *The Sexual Face of Violence: Rapists on Rape.* Johannesburg: Ravan Press, 1990.

Were, Gideon S., and Simiyu Wandibba, eds. *Meru District Socio-Cultural Profile.* Nairobi, Kenya: Government of Kenya and University of Nairobi (Classic Printers & Stationers Ltd.), 1988.

Women's International Network News. "Rape and Murder at Kenyan Catholic Boarding School in Meru." 17:4 (1991): 37–41.

Women, Men and Media Project. *Slipping from the Scene: News Coverage of Females Drops.* Alexandria, Va.: Unabridged Communications, 1995.

World Bank. *World Development Report 1991: The Challenge of Development.* New York: Oxford Univ. Press, 1991.

Worthington, Nancy. "Classifying Kenyan Women: Press Representations of Gender in Nairobi's 'Daily Nation.'" *Women's Studies in Communication* 18:1 (spring 1995): 65–84.

Yang, Shuchiao E. "Critical Approaches to the Study of Women's Magazines: A Review and Case Study of 'Singleness' in The Woman." Master's thesis, University of Oregon, 1993.

Yin, Robert K. *Case Study Research: Design and Methods.* Beverly Hills, Calif.: Sage, 1984.

Zoonen, Liesbet van. *Feminist Media Studies.* London: Sage, 1994.

Index

Adagala, Esther, 147n16
Africa: gender stereotypes about, 62, 82, 93, 99; global prejudices about, 57, 61, 94; political power in, 151n37; Western news traditions and, 156n10. *See also* East Africa
African Association for Women's Research and Development (AAWORD), 152n41, 174n17
African Women Development and Communication Network (Femnet), 152n41
Aga Kahn, Sadruddin, 23, 154n3
Agence France Press (AFP), 46, 53, 81, 82
Althusser, Louis, 3–4, 7, 97
Amnesty International, 19, 151n37
Anderson, Perry, 145, n1, 4
Anyanzwa, Fatuma Abeya, 91, 92, 173–74n17, 175n18
Apollos, Francis Macharia: academic credentials of, 164n32; on "accidental" killings, 170n72; on Meru violence, 59, 164n33; Perlez quotation of, 165n38; on rehabilitated boys, 157n24; Riithi quotation of, 59, 60
Aringo, Peter Oloo, 50, 51, 161n12, 163n19
Associated Press, 169n63
Association of Sisterhoods of Kenya (AOSK), 88
Awori, Horace, 161nn10, 11

Beijing Conference on Women (1995), 12, 149n26
Beijing Declaration and Platform for Action, 12
Benedict, Helen, 10, 26; bias identified by, 25; on male reporters, 38–39; on race/ethnicity, 56–57, 62, 171n87; recommendations by, 100–101; on victim identification, 70
Boserup, Ester, 151n38
British Broadcasting Corporation (BBC), 166n40, 169n63
British education, 32
British law, 19
Brownmiller, Susan, 149n30

Canadian law, 87
Catholic Church. *See* Roman Catholic Church
CBS News, 24–25
Central Park jogger rape (1989), 62, 164n26, 171n87
Chazan, David, 53–54, 161n12, 162n14
Chibnall, Steve, 146n11, 162n14
Chicago Tribune, 46, 62, 81, 82
Christianity, 17, 68. *See also* Roman Catholic Church
Christian Science Monitor, 81
Ciampa, Pio, 68
Consolata Catholic Church (Westlands), 90
Cullum-Swan, Betsy, 153n1

Daily Nation, 23, 76, 77, 103–6, 154–55n3; article placement in,

185

35; on assailants, 74–75, 157n24, 170n71, 171n88; early accounts by, 42, 43, 45; on educators, 51; on gender separation, 66; on immorality, 67; investigation demanded by, 47; on KMYWO, 88–89; labels used by, 79–83; on legal proceedings, 36; on Maendeleo House meeting, 91; on mixed schools, 65; Moi on, 54; on rape, 46, 49; reporter gender at, 35; space devoted by, 37; on stress, 55; on subversive elements, 50; on transferred students, 84–85; victims named by, 71, 78; on violence, 173n10; Worthington study of, 8–9. See also *Sunday Nation*
Declaration of Vienna and Program of Action, 12
Dow, Bonnie, 9
Dyer, Carolyn Stewart, 168n62, p149n29

East Africa, 29
"8-4-4" educational system, 32, 40, 53–56, 67, 161n10
Entman, Robert M., 155n6
Esipisu, Manoah, 46
Europe, 9, 28

Fair, Jo Ellen, 167n41
Farstad, Elizabeth, 10, 25, 155n8
Federal Bureau of Investigation (FBI), 153n43
Femnet, 152n41
Fiske, John, 63, 100
Fourth World Conference on Women (Beijing: 1995), 12, 149n26

Gacheru, Margareta wa, 174–75n17
Gallagher, Margaret, 146–47n16
Gans, Herbert, 158n27
Gitlin, Todd, 6, 24–25, 146n11, 153n1, 155n6
Glasgow Media Group, 155–56n8
Goffman, Erving, 155n5
Goldsmith, Paul, 29, 31, 156n12
Goretti, Maria, 68
Goro, Victoria N., 8
Gramsci, Antonio, 4, 6, 97, 145n1

Griffin, Susan, 134

Hachton, William, A. 156n10
Hall, Stuart, 7, 24, 146n15
Heise, Lori, 94, 175n23
Hirsch, Susan, 148n23
Holy Family Basilica (Nairobi), 175n18
Human Rights Conference (Vienna: 1993), 11

Igembe clan, 29, 57, 58
Imanyara, Gitobu, 53–54, 161n12
Imathiu, Imanene, 49, 75, 165–66n39, 171n88
Institute for Women, Law, and Development, 11–12
International Federation of Women Lawyers, 91
Inter Press Service, 94, 161nn10, 11, 175n23
Iraq, 9

Jaggar, Allison, 146n13

Kamau, Cecilia, 99; on KMYWO-KBPWO statement, 89, 93, 131–33; on memorial service, 90, 165n38
Kamweru, Esther, 77, 139–44, 159n35
Kangaru High School, 86
Kangeta, 57
Karambu, Viola, 71
Karanja, Mugambi, 59, 164n33
Karauri, Mathew Adams, 52, 165n38
Karimi, M., 80
Kendo, Oketch, 87, 125–27
Kenya African National Union (KANU): dissatisfaction with, 32; international press and, 50; Nakuru branch of, 92, 175n18; newspapers owned by, 23, 155n3. *See also* Maendeleo ya Wanawake Organization (MYWO)
Kenya Broadcasting Corporation (KBC), 155n3
Kenya Business and Professional Women's Organization (KBPWO), 46, 89–90, 152n41, 174n17 *Kenya Leo*, 154n3
Kenya Medical Association (KMA), 55

Kenya Ministry of Cultural and Social
Services Women's Bureau,
152n41, 153n42, 174n17
Kenya Ministry of Education, 51,
150–51n37
Kenya National Anti–Rape Organiza-
tion (KENARO), 91, 173–74n17,
175n18
Kenya National Game Reserve, 36
Kenya National Union of Teachers
(KNUT), 51
Kenya News Agency (KNA), 46, 75,
166n40
Kenya Nurses Association, 174n17
Kenya Power and Lighting Co., 50
Kenya Provincial Education Officers
(PEOS), 88
Kenya Secondary School Heads Association, 51, 57
Kenya Times, 23, 110–12, 154–55n3; on
academic performance, 172n6;
article placement in, 35; assailants named by, 76; early accounts by, 43, 45; on 8–4–4
system, 55; feminist perspectives
in, 92; on gender relations, 65; on
government critics, 161n12; government sources and, 48; labels
used by, 79–83, 171n87; on Laibon girl, 165n39; on legal proceedings, 36; on memorial
service, 90; on mixed schools,
65–66; Moi on, 54; on rape, 46,
57, 117–24; reporter gender at,
35; Riithi colleague at, 166n39;
on sexual morality, 68; space devoted by, 37, 38; on subversive
elements, 50; on team investigation, 49; victims named by, 71; on
violence, 58, 88; on women's organizations, 89, 93, 131–33,
174n17. See also *Sunday Times*
Kenya Women Organizing Committee
of the Women Individuals,
Groups and Organizations
against Abuse and Violence, 90
Kiai, Wambui, 147n16
Kibaki, Mwai, 53
Kibe, S. K., 51, 52, 57
Kikuyu clan, 18, 54, 92
King'ori, Marianne, 66

Kiriani Secondary School, 45
Kithira, Joyce: demotion of, 51; on
rape, 59, 60, 93, 94; name
spelling and title of, 162n15
Kizito, St., 68
Kuwait, 9
Kyungu, Sammy, 172n1

Laibon, Rose, 165n39, 166n39
Laiboni, James: appointment of, 33; denial by, 61, 166n40; dismissal of,
51; on drug addicts, 82; ethnicity
of, 57–58; name spelling of,
157n22; on mixed schools,
64–65; Riithi quotation of, 59–60
Landsberg, Michele, 93–94, 99,
136–38, 172n6, 175n22
Lang, Gretchen, 168n54
Levinson, David, 13, 16
LEXIS/NEXIS, 2, 23, 113–16, 154n2;
early accounts in, 46; labels in,
81, 171n84; photographic information in, 169n64; primary
sources in, 53
London *Times*, 81
Lonrho Corporation, 23, 77,
154–55n3, 170n78
Los Angeles Times, 81
Luo clan, 18
Luseno, Evans, 174n17
Lyman, Stanford M., 156n10

Maasai Mara, 36
MacKinnon, Catherine A., 148n20
McCarthy, Sheryl, 62, 93
Maendeleo ya Wanawake Organization
(MYWO), 88–90, 152n41
Malembe, Joseph, 50
Maja-Pearce, Adewale, 154n3
Manning, Peter K., 153n1
Mary Tyler Moore Show, 9
Masinde, Philip, 161n11
Mbogo, Julius, 172n1
Mbugguss, Martha, 91
Meru ethnic group, 29; alleged vio-
lence of, 40, 99–100, 164n33,
165n38, 166n39; frustration of,
54; prejudice against, 57, 98; val-
ues of, 31, 56, 61
Meru District, 27, 29; clannism in, 58;
girls' schools in, 85; prison in,

74–75; public opinion in, 167n52; violence in, 59
Meru District Hospital, 34, 43, 71
Meru National Park, 29
Mills, Kay, 159n37
Mkanju (writer), 88, 129–30
Moi, Daniel T. arap: on "black sheep," 82; on indiscipline, 43, 45, 47; Kithira and, 60; KMYWO and, 89; media castigated by, 54; on mixed schools, 64; personal visit by, 48–49; son of, 155n3, 170n78; team appointed by, 51; transfer decision and, 85
Montreal murders (1989), 87, 90
Mothers in Action (organization), 86, 91, 92, 172n6, 174n17
Mouffe, Chantal, 4, 145–46n4
Mpaka, Christine, 172n6
Mugo, Beth, 46, 90
Muluka–Lutta, Sophie A., 8
Mungatia, Andrew, 65, 167n52
Musungu, Willis Tsuma, 66
Mutahi, Wahome, 173n10
Mutere, Absalom, 159n35
Muya, Wamahiu, 57, 58
Mwanga, Kabaka, 68
Mwangi, Julius, 51, 58
Mwangi, Wagaki, 8

Nairobi, 18, 27
Nairobi press. See *Daily Nation*; *Kenya Times*; *Standard, The*; *Weekly Review*
Nairobi Primary School Heads Association, 51, 58
Nation. See *Daily Nation*
National Council of Women of Kenya, 152n41
National Game Reserve, 36
Nation Group of Newspapers, 154n3
Ndirangu, Irungu, 165n38
New Bedford rape (1983), 10, 90, 164n26
Newsday, 46, 62, 81, 82
New York jogger rape (1989), 62, 164n26, 171n87
New York Times: on Kenyan women, 93; on Kuwait invasion, 9; labels used by, 81; on mixed schools, 66; on St. Kizito, 46; on SDS, 24–25
NEXIS. *See* LEXIS/NEXIS

Ng'weno, Hilary, 88, 93, 98, 128
Njoroge, Mwicigi, 65
Njoya, Rev., 173n10
Njue, John, 54
North America, 28
Now, 170n78
Nyambene clan, 29, 31, 156n12
Nzomo, Maria, 151n37, 152–53n41

Obura, Anne, 8
Ochieng, Philip, 37, 38, 159n32, 161n12, 166n39
Odero, Norbert, 67
Okie, Susan, 94, 175n23
Okoth, Zaccheus, 67–68
Omangi, Daniel, 84–85
Ombonya (judge), 74
Onsando, Wilkista, 90
Orlando Sentinel Tribune, 46
Otani, Robert, 65–66
Otieno, S. M., 18
Otieno, Wambui, 18
Ottowa Citizen, 81
Otunga, Maurice, 77, 92, 175n18

Palm Beach rape (1991), 62, 168n61
Pathak, Zakia, 152n39
Pauley, John, 154n2
Perlez, Jane, 66, 93, 164n32, 165n38
Polk, Glenda C., 15–16
Portuguese Americans, 164n26
Provincial Education Officers (PEOS), 88
Public Law Institute, 153n42

Reuters (news agency), 46, 81, 82
Riithi, Alex: audience exploitation of, 63; early account by, 45; international quotation of, 166–67n40; on jealous boys, 71, 73; Karanja and, 164n33; on Laibon girl, 165n39; Perlez quotation of, 165n38; on rape, 59–60, 93, 117–24; reliability of, 61, 166n39; on suspects, 76; mentioned, 89, 94
Roman Catholic Church, 32, 64, 67–68, 161n12. *See also* Consolata Catholic Church (Westlands); Holy Family Basilica (Nairobi)
Rozee-Koker, Patricia A., 15–16

Rugene, Catherine Njeri, 8
Ruigu, George M., 150n36, 151n37

Sagini, Lawrence, 49–50
St. Cyprian school, 34
St. John's incident, 62
St. Petersburg Times, 46
Saisi, Peter, 47, 54
Salvini, Catherine, 66
Sanday, Peggy Reeves, 13, 16
Sitima, Tom, 88, 172n1
Smith, William Kennedy, 62, 168n61
Steeves, H. Leslie, 146n13; 151–52n38
Some, Jane, 66
Stamp, Patricia, 18, 78, 152n39
Standard, The, 23, 107–9, 154–55n3,
    159n35; on AOSK, 88; article
    placement in, 35; assailants
    named by, 76–77, 78; "concerned
    parent" and, 52; early accounts
    by, 45; on 8–4–4 system, 53; fem-
    inist perspectives in, 92; on gov-
    ernment policy, 67; on
    KMYWO-KBPWO statement,
    89; labels used by, 79–83; on
    legal proceedings, 36; on op-
    pressed women, 91; patients in-
    terviewed by, 47; purchase of,
    170n78; on rape, 46; reporter
    gender at, 35; on sexism, 87,
    125–27; space devoted by, 37; on
    subversive elements, 50; on
    transferred students, 85; victims
    named in, 71. See also *Sunday
    Standard*
Staudt, Kathleen, 151n37, 152n39
Students for a Democratic Society
    (SDS), 24–25
Sunday Nation, 23, 106–7; on academic
    performance, 34, 172n6; article
    placement in, 35; on ethnicity,
    57–58; on gender violence, 88,
    129–30; on immorality, 67; on
    Laibon girl, 165n39, 166n39; on
    legal aid clinic, 174–75n17; on
    mixed schools, 64–65; on Moth-
    ers in Action, 86, 172n6; on
    North American rapes, 90–91,
    134–35; on Otunga, 77, 139–44;
    reporter gender at, 35; space de-
    voted by, 37; on stress, 55
Sunday Standard, 23, 109; article place-

ment in, 35; entertainment maga-
    zine of, 170n78; reporter gender
    at, 35; space devoted by, 37
Sunday Times, 23, 112; article place-
    ment in, 35; reporter gender at,
    35; space devoted by, 37; on vio-
    lence, 58–59, 164n33
Sunder Rajan, Rajeswari, 152n39

Taifa Leo, 154n3
Taiwan, 9
Tharamba, Mercy, 169n66
Tigania clan, 29, 58, 165n38
Tigania Mission Hospital, 34, 47, 71
Tigania stadium, 49
Time, 81
Times, The (London), 81
Too, Mark, 155n3, 170n78
Toronto Star, 93–94, 99, 136–38, 172n6
Tuchman, Gaye, 99, 146n11, 155n5
Tyson rape trial (1992), 36–37,
    158n30

United Nations Children's Fund,
    175n22
United Nations Development Fund for
    Women, 12, 149n25
United Nations Fourth World Confer-
    ence on Women (Beijing: 1995),
    12, 149n26
United Nations Human Rights Con-
    ference (Vienna: 1993), 11
United States: criminal code of,
    153n43; educational system of,
    32; press of, 9, 100, 148n23,
    155n6; rape in, 10, 14, 16, 100,
    148n23 (*See also* Central Park
    jogger rape (1989); New Bedford
    rape (1983); Palm Beach rape
    (1991); Tyson rape trial (1992));
    victim identification in, 68, 70
United States Federal Bureau of Inves-
    tigation, 153n43
University of Nairobi Council, 49–50
USA Today, 46

Vancouver Sun, 81
Vidich, Arthur, 156n10
Vienna Human Rights Conference
    (1993), 11
Vietnam War, 24–25

Wahome, James, 66
Waithaka, James, 51
Wandibba, Simiyu, 156n12
Warah, Rasna, 90–91, 99, 134–35
Ward, Julie, 36, 158n30
Washington Post, 62, 94
Washington Times, 46
Weekly Review, 23, 98, 112–13; article
   placement in, 35; on assailants,
   76, 78; feminist perspectives in,
   92; on indiscipline committee,
   161n10; on mixed schools, 66; reporter gender at, 35; on sexism,
   88, 91, 93, 128; victims named in,
   70, 71
Were, Gideon S., 156n12
Western countries: African stereotypes of, 62, 93, 99; feminist
   study of, 97; journalistic training
   in, 27–28; news traditions of,
   156n10; values of, 17

Women, Men and Media project,
   147n16
Women's Bureau of Kenya, 152n41,
   153n42, 174n17
Women's International Network News, 93
Women's Legal Aid Clinic, 91,
   174–75n17
Workshop on Gender and Human
   Rights, 11–12
World Conference on Women (Beijing:
   1995), 12, 149n26
Worthington, Nancy, 8–9

Yang, Shuchiao, 9

Zoonen, Liesbet van, 22, 28, 146n14

Monographs in International Studies

Titles Available from Ohio University Press, 1997

Southeast Asia Series

No. 56   Duiker, William J. Vietnam Since the Fall of Saigon. 1989.
Updated ed. 401 pp. Paper 0-89680-162-4 $20.00.

No. 64   Dardjowidjojo, Soenjono. Vocabulary Building in Indonesian:
An Advanced Reader. 1984. 664 pp. Paper 0-89680-118-7
$30.00.

No. 65   Errington, J. Joseph. Language and Social Change in Java:
Linguistic Reflexes of Modernization in a Traditional Royal
Polity. 1985. 210 pp. Paper 0-89680-120-9 $25.00.

No. 66   Binh, Tran Tu. The Red Earth: A Vietnamese Memoir of Life
on a Colonial Rubber Plantation. Tr. by John Spragens. 1984.
102 pp. (SEAT*, V. 5) Paper 0-89680-119-5 $11.00.

No. 68   Syukri, Ibrahim. History of the Malay Kingdom of Patani.
1985. 135 pp. Paper 0-89680-123-3 $15.00.

No. 69   Keeler, Ward. Javanese: A Cultural Approach. 1984. 559 pp.
Paper 0-89680-121-7 $25.00.

No. 70   Wilson, Constance M. and Lucien M. Hanks. Burma-Thai-
land Frontier Over Sixteen Decades: Three Descriptive Documents. 1985. 128 pp. Paper 0-89680-124-1 $11.00.

No. 71   Thomas, Lynn L. and Franz von Benda-Beckmann, eds.
Change and Continuity in Minangkabau: Local, Regional, and
Historical Perspectives on West Sumatra. 1985. 353 pp. Paper
0-89680-127-6 $16.00.

No. 72   Reid, Anthony and Oki Akira, eds. The Japanese Experience
in Indonesia: Selected Memoirs of 1942–1945. 1986. 424 pp.,
20 illus. (SEAT, V. 6) Paper 0-89680-132-2 $20.00.

* Southeast Asia Translation Project Group

No. 74   **McArthur M. S. H.** Report on Brunei in 1904. Introduced and Annotated by A. V. M. Horton. 1987. 297 pp. Paper 0-89680-135-7 $15.00.

No. 75   **Lockard, Craig A.** From Kampung to City: A Social History of Kuching, Malaysia, 1820–1970. 1987. 325 pp. Paper 0-89680-136-5 $20.00.

No. 76   **McGinn, Richard,** ed. Studies in Austronesian Linguistics. 1986. 516 pp. Paper 0-89680-137-3 $20.00.

No. 77   **Muego, Benjamin N.** Spectator Society: The Philippines Under Martial Rule. 1986. 232 pp. Paper 0-89680-138-1 $17.00.

No 79   **Walton, Susan Pratt.** Mode in Javanese Music. 1987. 278 pp. Paper 0-89680-144-6 $15.00.

No. 80   **Nguyen Anh Tuan.** South Vietnam: Trial and Experience. 1987. 477 pp., tables. Paper 0-89680-141-1 $18.00.

No. 82   **Spores, John C.** Running Amok: An Historical Inquiry. 1988. 190 pp. paper 0-89680-140-3 $13.00.

No. 83   **Malaka, Tan.** From Jail to Jail. Tr. by Helen Jarvis. 1911. 1209 pp., three volumes. (SEAT V. 8) Paper 0-89680-150-0 $55.00.

No. 84   **Devas, Nick, with Brian Binder, Anne Booth, Kenneth Davey, and Roy Kelly.** Financing Local Government in Indonesia. 1989. 360 pp. Paper 0-89680-153-5 $20.00.

No. 85   **Suryadinata, Leo.** Military Ascendancy and Political Culture: A Study of Indonesia's Golkar. 1989. 235 pp., illus., glossary, append., index, bibliog. Paper 0-89680-154-3 $18.00.

No. 86   **Williams, Michael.** Communism, Religion, and Revolt in Banten in the Early Twentieth Century. 1990. 390 pp. Paper 0-89680-155-1 $14.00.

No. 87   **Hudak, Thomas.** The Indigenization of Pali Meters in Thai Poetry. 1990. 247 pp. Paper 0-89680-159-4 $15.00.

No. 88   **Lay, Ma Ma.** Not Out of Hate: A Novel of Burma. Tr. by Margaret Aung-Thwin. Ed. by William Frederick. 1991. 260 pp. (SEAT V. 9) Paper 0-89680-167-5 $20.00.

No. 89   **Anwar, Chairil.** The Voice of the Night: Complete Poetry and Prose of Chairil Anwar. 1992. Revised Edition. Tr. by Burton Raffel. 196 pp. Paper 0-89680-170-5 $20.00.

No. 90   **Hudak, Thomas John,** tr., The Tale of Prince Samuttakote: A Buddhist Epic from Thailand. 1993. 230 pp. Paper 0-89680-174-8 $20.00.

No. 91   **Roskies, D. M.,** ed. Text/Politics in Island Southeast Asia:

Essays in Interpretation. 1993. 330 pp. Paper 0-89680-175-6 $25.00.

No. 92   Schenkhuizen, Marguérite, translated by Lizelot Stout van Balgooy. Memoirs of an Indo Woman: Twentieth-Century Life in the East Indies and Abroad. 1993. 312 pp. Paper 0-89680-178-0 $25.00.

No. 93   Salleh, Muhammad Haji. Beyond the Archipelago: Selected Poems. 1995. 247 pp. Paper 0-89680-181-0 $20.00.

No. 94   Federspiel, Howard M. A Dictionary of Indonesian Islam. 1995. 327 pp. Bibliog. Paper 0-89680-182-9 $25.00.

No. 95   Leary, John. Violence and the Dream People: The Orang Asli in the Malayan Emergency 1948–1960. 1995. 275 pp. Maps, illus., tables, appendices, bibliog., index. Paper 0-89680-186-1 $22.00.

No. 96   Lewis, Dianne. *Jan Compagnie* in the Straits of Malacca 1641–1795. 1995. 176 pp. Map, appendices, bibliog., index. Paper 0-89680-187-x. $18.00.

No. 97   Schiller, Jim and Martin-Schiller, Barbara. Imagining Indonesia: Cultural Politics and Political Culture. 1996. 384 pp., notes, glossary, bibliog. Paper 0-89680-190-x. $30.00.

No. 98   Bonga, Dieuwke Wendelaar. Eight Prison Camps: A Dutch Family in Japanese Java. 1996. 233 pp., illus., map, glossary. Paper 0-89680-191-8. $18.00.

No. 99   Gunn, Geoffrey C. Language, Ideology, and Power in Brunei Darussalam. 1996. 328 pp., glossary, notes, bibliog., index. Paper 0-86980-192-6 $24.00.

No. 100   Martin, Peter W., Conrad Ozog, and Gloria R. Poedjosoedarmo, eds. Language Use and Language Change in Brunei Darussalam. 1996. 390 pp., maps, notes, bibliog. Paper 0-89680-193-4. $26.00.

Africa Series

No. 43   Harik, Elsa M. and Donald G. Schilling. The Politics of Education in Colonial Algeria and Kenya. 1984. 102 pp. Paper 0-89680-117-9 $12.50.

No. 45   Keto, C. Tsehloane. American-South African Relations 1784–1980: Review and Select Bibliography. 1985. 169 pp. Paper 0-89680-128-4 $11.00.

No. 46 Burness, Don, ed. Wanasema: Conversations with African Writers. 1985. 103 pp. paper 0-89680-129-2 $11.00.

No. 47 Switzer, Les. Media and Dependency in South Africa: A Case Study of the Press and the Ciskei "Homeland." 1985. 97 pp. Paper 0-89680-130-6 $10.00.

No. 51 Clayton, Anthony and David Killingray. Khaki and Blue: Military and Police in British Colonial Africa. 1989. 347 pp. Paper 0-89680-147-0 $20.00.

No. 52 Northrup, David. Beyond the Bend in the River: African Labor in Eastern Zaire, 1865–1940. 1988. 282 pp. Paper 0-89680-151-9 $15.00.

No. 53 Makinde, M. Akin. African Philosophy, Culture, and Traditional Medicine. 1988. 172 pp. Paper 0-89680-152-7 $16.00.

No. 54 Parson, Jack, ed. Succession to High Office in Botswana: Three Case Studies. 1990. 455 pp. Paper 0-89680-157-8 $20.00.

No. 56 Staudinger, Paul. In the Heart of the Hausa States. Tr. by Johanna E. Moody. Foreword by Paul Lovejoy. 1990. In two volumes., 469 + 224 pp., maps, apps. Paper 0-89680-160-8 (2 vols.) $35.00.

No. 57 Sikainga, Ahmad Alawad. The Western Bahr Al-Ghazal under British Rule, 1898–1956. 1991. 195 pp. Paper 0-89680-161-6 $15.00.

No. 58 Wilson, Louis E. The Krobo People of Ghana to 1892: A Political and Social History. 1991. 285 pp. Paper 0-89680-164-0 $20.00.

No. 59 du Toit, Brian M. Cannabis, Alcohol, and the South African Student: Adolescent Drug Use, 1974–1985. 1991. 176 pp., notes, tables. Paper 0-89680-166-7 $17.00.

No. 60 Falola, Toyin and Dennis Itavyar, eds. The Political Economy of Health in Africa. 1992. 258 pp., notes, tables. Paper 0-89680-166-7 $20.00.

No. 61 Kiros, Tedros. Moral Philosophy and Development: The Human Condition in Africa. 1992. 199 pp., notes. Paper 0-89680-171-3 $20.00.

No. 62 Burness, Don. Echoes of the Sunbird: An Anthology of Contemporary African Poetry. 1993. 198 pp. Paper 0-89680-173-x $17.00.

No. 64 Nelson, Samuel H. Colonialism in the Congo Basin 1880–1940. 1994. 290 pp. Index. Paper 0-89680-180-2 $23.00.

No. 66 Ilesanmi, Simeon Olusegun. Religious Pluralism and the

Nigerian State. 1996. 336 pp., maps, notes, bibliog., index.
Paper 0-89680-194-2 $23.00.

No. 67   Steeves, H. Leslie. Gender Violence and the Press: The St.
Kizito Story. 1997. 176 pp., illus., notes, bibliog., index. Paper
0-89680195-0 $17.95.

Latin America Series

No. 9   Tata, Robert J. Structural Changes in Puerto Rico's Economy: 1947–1976. 1981. 118 pp. paper 0-89680-107-1 $12.00.

No. 13   Henderson, James D. Conservative Thought in Latin America: The Ideas of Laureano Gomez. 1988. 229 pp. Paper 0-
89680-148-9 $16.00.

No. 17   Mijeski, Kenneth J., ed. The Nicaraguan Constitution of
1987: English Translation and Commentary. 1991. 355 pp.
Paper 0-89680-165-9 $25.00.

No. 18   Finnegan, Pamela. The Tension of Paradox: José Donoso's
The Obscene Bird of Night as Spiritual Exercises. 1992. 204 pp.
Paper 0-89680-169-1 $15.00.

No. 19   Kim, Sung Ho and Thomas W. Walker, eds. Perspectives on
War and Peace in Central America. 1992. 155 pp., notes, bibliog. Paper 0-89680-172-1 $17.00.

No. 20   Becker, Marc. Mariátegui and Latin American Marxist Theory. 1993. 239 pp. Paper 0-89680-177-2 $20.00.

No. 21   Boschetto-Sandoval, Sandra M. and Marcia Phillips Mc-
Gowan, eds. Claribel Alegría and Central American Literature. 1994. 233 pp., illus. Paper 0-89680-179-9 $20.00.

No. 22   Zimmerman, Marc. Literature and Resistance in Guatemala:
Textual Modes and Cultural Politics from El Señor Presi-
dente to Rigoberta Menchú. 1995. 2 volume set 320 + 370 pp.,
notes, bibliog. Paper 0-89680-183-7 $50.00.

No. 23   Hey, Jeanne A. K. Theories of Dependent Foreign Policy:
The Case of Ecuador in the 1980s. 1995. 280 pp., map, tables,
notes, bibliog., index. paper 0-89680-184-5 $22.00.

No. 24   Wright, Bruce E. Theory in the Practice of the Nicaraguan
Revolution. 1995. 320 pp., notes, illus., bibliog., index. Paper 0-
89680-185-3. $23.00.

No. 25   Mann, Carlos Guevara. Panamanian Militarism: A Historical
Interpretation. 1996. 243 pp., illus., map, notes, bibliog., index.
Paper 0-89680-189-6 $23.00.

No. 26   Armony, Ariel. Argentina, the United States, and the Anti-Communist Crusade in Central America. 1997. 305 pp. (est.) illus., maps, notes, bibliog., index. Paper 0-89680-196-9 $26.00.

Ordering Information

Individuals are encouraged to patronize local bookstores wherever possible. Orders for titles in the Monographs in International Studies may be placed directly through the Ohio University Press, Scott Quadrangle, Athens, Ohio 45701-2979. Individuals should remit payment by check, VISA, or MasterCard.* Those ordering from the United Kingdom, Continental Europe, the Middle East, and Africa should order through Academic and University Publishers Group, 1 Gower Street, London WC1E, England. Orders from the Pacific Region, Asia, Australia, and New Zealand should be sent to East-West Export Books, c/o the University of Hawaii Press, 2840 Kolowalu Street, Honolulu, Hawaii 96822, USA.

Individuals ordering from outside of the U.S. should remit in U.S. funds to Ohio University Press either by International Money Order or by a check drawn on a U.S. bank.** Most out-of-print titles may be ordered from University Microfilms, Inc., 300 North Zeeb Road, Ann Arbor, Michigan 48106, USA.

Prices are subject to change.

* Please add $3.50 for the first book and $.75 for each additional book for shipping and handling.

** Outside the U.S. please add $4.50 for the first book and $.75 for each additional book.

Ohio University
Center for International Studies

The Ohio University Center for International Studies was established to help create within the university and local communities a greater awareness of the world beyond the United States. Comprising programs in African, Latin American, Southeast Asian, Development and Administrative studies, the Center supports scholarly research, sponsors lectures and colloquia, encourages course development within the university curriculum, and publishes the Monographs in International Studies series with the Ohio University Press. The Center and its programs also offer an interdisciplinary Master of Arts degree in which students may focus on one of the regional or topical concentrations, and may also combine academics with training in career fields such as journalism, business, and language teaching. For undergraduates, major and certificate programs are also available.

For more information, contact the Vice Provost for International Studies, Burson House, Ohio University, Athens, Ohio 45701.